1,000+ Little Things
Happy, Successful People
Do Differently

1,000+ Little Things

Happy, Successful People Do Differently

MARC & ANGEL CHERNOFF

A TARCHERPERIGEE BOOK

tarcherperigee

An imprint of Penguin Random House LLC
penguinrandomhouse.com

Originally published in different form by the authors in 2013
Copyright © 2019 by Marc Chernoff and Angel Chernoff
Penguin supports copyright. Copyright fuels creativity, encourages diverse
voices, promotes free speech, and creates a vibrant culture. Thank you for buying
an authorized edition of this book and for complying with copyright laws by not
reproducing, scanning, or distributing any part of it in any form without
permission. You are supporting writers and allowing Penguin to continue
to publish books for every reader.

TarcherPerigee with tp colophon is a registered trademark of
Penguin Random House LLC.

Marc Chernoff and Angel Chernoff are available for select speaking
engagements. To inquire about a possible appearance, please contact Penguin
Random House Speakers Bureau at speakers@penguinrandomhouse.com or visit
www.prhspeakers.com.

Most TarcherPerigee books are available at special quantity discounts for
bulk purchase for sales promotions, premiums, fund-raising, and educational
needs. Special books or book excerpts also can be created to fit specific needs.
For details, write: SpecialMarkets@penguinrandomhouse.com.

Library of Congress Cataloging-in-Publication Data
Names: Chernoff, Marc, author. | Chernoff, Angel, author.
Title: 1000+ little things happy successful people do differently /
Marc Chernoff, Angel Chernoff.
Other titles: One thousand plus little things happy successful
people do differently
Description: New York : TarcherPerigee, 2019.
Identifiers: LCCN 2019005255| ISBN 9780525542742 (hardback) |
ISBN 9780525504689 (ebook)
Subjects: LCSH: Success. | Happiness. | BISAC: SELF-HELP / Personal Growth /
Success. | SELF-HELP / Personal Growth / Happiness. | SELF-HELP /
Motivational & Inspirational.
Classification: LCC BF637.S8 C4684 2019 | DDC 158.1—dc23
LC record available at https://lccn.loc.gov/2019005255

Printed in the United States of America
5 7 9 10 8 6 4

Interior art: Memphis patterns by ExpressVectors /
Shutterstock.com; Sunburst by WANWIDesign /
Shutterstock.com

Book design by Kristin del Rosario

To our students, friends, and family
who inspire us every day

Contents

Introduction

MILLIONS OF PEOPLE live their entire lives on default settings, never realizing they can customize everything. Don't be one of them. Don't settle for the default settings in life.

Dare to make edits and improvements. Dare to make your personal growth a top priority.

The truth is, you won't always be a priority to others, and that's why you need to be a priority to yourself. Learn to respect yourself, take care of yourself, and become your own support system. Your needs matter. Start meeting them!

Don't wait on others to choose you. Choose yourself today!

Seriously, it's not your job to curb or contain yourself in order to become someone else's idea of a worthwhile human being. You are amazingly worthwhile and capable right now. Not because other people think you are, but because you are in full control of the next step you take.

If you feel differently, or if you've been holding yourself back recently, realize that the real battle is in your mind. And your mind is under your control, not the other way around. You may have been broken down by adversity or rejection or stress, but *you* are not broken. So don't let your mind, or anyone else, try to convince you otherwise.

Heal yourself, and grow beyond the default settings in life, by refusing to settle for the way things have always been. Choose to take up a lot of positive space in your own life today. Choose to give yourself permission to meet your own needs. Choose to honor your feelings and emotions. Choose to make self-care and personal growth top priorities . . .

Choose to think better about yourself, so that you can live better in spite of the challenges you face.

And *yes*, we know that's sometimes much easier said than done. Making positive changes takes guidance and practice. And that's exactly what this book will help you achieve, one tiny step at a time.

Are you ready for a great journey? Achieving real happiness and success in life is truly a wild one—a journey of unexpected and exciting twists, turns, and vital lessons. Yes, it's wild how we outgrow what we once thought we couldn't live without, and then we fall in love with what we didn't even know we wanted. Life keeps leading us down paths we would never travel if it were up to us. Don't be afraid. Don't let your expectations of how everything "should be" blind you to the beauty of the life you're living. Have faith. Trust the journey.

And of course, if you're struggling with trusting the journey and taming your expectations right now, know that you are not alone. Many of us are here with you, working hard to let go, find more presence and acceptance, and get our thinking back on track. Let us share a quick metaphor with you that we often share with our course students and live seminar attendees:

Imagine you had a ripe, juicy tangerine sitting on the table in front of you. You pick it up eagerly, take a bite, and begin to taste it.

You already know how a ripe, juicy tangerine should taste, and so when this one is a bit tarter than expected, you make a face, feel a sense of disappointment, and swallow it, feeling cheated out of the experience you expected.

Or perhaps the tangerine tastes completely normal—nothing special at all. So, you swallow it without even pausing to appreciate its flavor as you move on to the next unworthy bite, and the next.

In the first scenario, the tangerine let you down because it didn't meet your expectations. In the second, it was too plain because it met your expectations to a T.

Do you see the irony here?

It's either not good or not good enough. This is how many of us live our lives . . . unhappily and unsuccessfully. It's why so many of us feel let down, disappointed, and unexcited about almost everything.

Because nothing *really* meets our expectations.

Now, imagine you try this instead: remove your expectations of how the tangerine "should" taste. You don't know, and you don't expect to know, because you haven't even tried it yet. Instead, you're genuinely curious, impartial, and open to a variety of possible flavors. You taste it, and you truly pay attention. You notice the juiciness, the texture of the pulp, the simultaneously tangy, tart, and sweet flavors swirling around on your tongue, and all the other complex sensations that arise in your awareness as you chew. You didn't know how this tangerine would taste, but now you realize it's different from the rest, and it's remarkable in its own way. It's a totally new experience—a worthwhile experience—because you've never tasted *this* tangerine before.

Mindfulness experts often refer to this as "beginner's mind," but really, it's just the result of a mind-set free of needless, stifling expectations.

The tangerine, of course, can be substituted for almost anything in your life: any event, any situation, any relationship, any person, any thought at all that enters your mind. If you approach any of these with expectations of "how it should be" or "how it has to be" in order to be good enough for you, they will almost always disappoint you in some way, or be too plain and unexciting to even remember. And you'll just move on to the next disappointment or unworthy life experience, and the next, and the next, and so on and so forth, until you've lived the vast majority of your life stuck in an endless cycle of experiences you barely like or barely even notice.

A Better Way

The good news is, there is a happier and more successful way to think and live. When we add up more than a decade's worth of one-on-one coaching sessions with students, open conversations with our readers, and the annual live seminars we host, we have lots of experience when it comes to assisting people through the pain points that have been holding them back. And one of the most prevalent pain points we've seen unfold over the years is what we've just discussed—expectations gone wrong. In fact, most of what we describe as our "biggest problems" are the direct consequence of how we react to life on an average day.

Yes, sometimes there are major tragedies to cope with, but most of the time the only real problem is our mind-set and resulting behavior in the present moment. Exercising your mental strength—your inner resilience—is key. And you don't have to be born mentally strong, either. You can develop this vital character trait with daily practice.

Is it easy? Not exactly. Is it worth it? Absolutely.

And it all starts with facing the present moment fully, with genuine presence and acceptance. Even when times are relatively good, one of the hardest challenges we face in life is to simply live in our own skin—to just be right here, right now, regardless of where we are. Too often we aimlessly distract ourselves with anything and everything: food, booze, shopping, television, gossip, news, social networks, video games, smartphones, tablets—anything to keep us from being fully present.

We use compulsive work, compulsive exercise, compulsive love affairs, and more to escape from ourselves and the realities of living with full presence. In fact, many of us will go to great lengths to avoid the feeling of being alone with ourselves in an undistracted way. For being alone means dealing with our true feelings: fears, anxieties, anticipation, uncertainty, frustration, envy, disappointment. And when harder times hit, things spiral even further out of control.

On the flip side, we can exercise our mental strength muscles and gradually grow to understand that finding peace, happiness, and success in life does not mean to be in a place where there is no noise, no hardship, and no unfinished business. It means to be in the midst of those things while remaining focused in your mind and calm in your heart. It's about letting go of the pictures in your head about how things were "supposed to be" and facing the present moment's challenges with presence and poise.

Presence Is Everything

Begin by noticing with curiosity, and without judgment, all the ways in which you avoid being in your own skin, with your own issues, right here, right now, in this present moment. Then focus, carefully, on what you're truly feeling. Don't numb yourself with distractions or expectations, but instead bring how you feel further into your awareness. Make yourself the number one priority of this moment.

Turn to the moment fully and welcome it. Smile, and give what you feel your full, thoughtful attention. Because if you don't allow yourself to move past what happened, what was said, what was felt, you will look at your present and future through that same dirty lens, and nothing will be able to focus your foggy judgment.

Bottom line: What you do now matters more than what happened yesterday. And what you do now is *your choice*.

Yes, it's your choice. And if you're choosing to complain, to blame, to be stuck in the past, to act like a victim, to feel anger, to ignore your intuition, to give up . . . then it's time to choose differently. Choose to do the little things you need to take a step forward in the present.

WHEN YOU TREAT the present moment with respect—when you respond to it effectively—you truly get the chance of a lifetime. Recently, we were reminded of this in the most beautiful way. We were sitting on a park bench near our home in South Florida, eating a picnic lunch, when an elderly couple pulled their car up under a nearby oak tree. They rolled down the windows and turned up some jazz music on the radio. Then the man got out of the car, walked around to the passenger side, helped the woman out of her seat, and guided her about ten feet away from the car. They slow-danced for the next half hour under the oak tree.

It was truly a sight to see. We could have watched them forever. And as they wrapped things up and started making their way back to the car, we clapped our hands in admiration.

The elderly couple slowly walked over to us with smiles on their faces. "Thank you for the applause," the woman chuckled.

"Thank *you*," Angel immediately replied. "You two dancing gives us hope."

They both smiled even wider as they looked at us. "Well, us dancing gives us hope too," the woman said as she grabbed the man's hand. "Because what you don't realize is that you just witnessed the power and beauty of second and third chances."

They went on to explain that they had each lost beloved spouses (in her case, two of them over the years). They had come together in marriage just three years earlier—kindred souls who found each other after what felt like losing everything.

Angel and I spent the next few days thinking about that beautiful couple, about second and third chances, and about how human beings find the motivation to keep going—to keep loving, to keep living in the present, despite the pain and grief and hopelessness and stress we all inevitably experience along the way. And this topic hits close to home too.

Our Story

A decade ago, in a relatively short time frame, we faced several significant, unexpected losses and life changes, back-to-back:

Losing a sibling to suicide. Losing our best friend to cardiac arrest. Financial uncertainty following a breadwinning-job loss. Breaking ties with a loved one who repeatedly betrayed us. Family business failure.

Those experiences were brutal. And enduring them in quick succession knocked us down and off course for a period of time. For example, when Angel's brother died, facing this reality while supporting her grieving family was incredibly painful at times. There were moments when we shut out the world and avoided our loved ones who were grieving alongside us. We didn't want to deal with the pain, so we coped by running away, by finding ways to numb ourselves with alcohol and unhealthy distractions. And consequently, we grew physically ill while the pain continued to fester inside us.

We felt terrible for far too long. And getting to the right state of mind—one that actually allowed us to physically and emotionally move forward again—required diligent practice. We had to learn to consciously free our minds, so that we could think straight and open ourselves to the present opportunities in front of us.

We learned that when you face struggles with an attitude of openness—open to the painful feelings and emotions you have—it's not comfortable, but you can step forward. Openness means you admit that you don't really know what the next step will be like, and you'd like to understand the whole truth of the matter. It's being fully present and willing to learn and grow.

One Step at a Time

The simplest way to initiate this mind-set shift? Little daily reminders.

It's all about keeping the right thoughts at the top of your mind, so they're readily available when you need them most. For us, especially when we were in the thick of things, that meant sitting down quietly with ourselves every morning and evening and reflecting on precisely what we needed to remember. We used short written reminders, which we've collected in this book, to do just that. Sometimes we'd call them mantras, or affirmations, or prayers, or convictions. These daily reminders kept us motivated and on track by helping us stay grounded, with peaceful, productive thoughts at the top of our minds, even when life got utterly chaotic.

And we've witnessed the power of this practice unfold time and again in other people's lives too—through our blog, workshops, and an earlier version of this book as well. We've heard powerful stories of readers facing serious health challenges and other potentially catastrophic issues. Their experiences are a reminder that even when harsh circumstances threaten to bring us down to the lowest of lows, we can keep our minds focused on the positive and our hearts open, and continue to put one foot in front of the other, to recover the pieces, rebuild, and fight back with more strength and determination than we ever imagined possible.

So, if you're currently struggling, hang in there. Sometimes the best thing that can happen to us in the long run is not getting exactly what we want right now. Make today the beginning of a new chance. Take time to be present with yourself. Take time to eliminate the old expectations getting in your way. Take time to love, laugh, cry, learn, and work for what you need right now. We hope the simple reminders in this book will help you find genuine peace and progress, no matter what you're facing. Digest a few pages at a time, mull over the ideas that move you, and gradually turn them into positive rituals in your life.

1,000+ Little Things
Happy, Successful People
Do Differently

PART ONE

· · · · ·

Happiness

*Wake up every morning with the idea that something
wonderful is possible today.*

OPENING OUR EYES

WE'VE HEARD SO many powerful stories of individuals shifting their perspective to see and feel the love that's all around them—to more fully experience the profound happiness that's already there, waiting to be accessed and fully *lived*. One example comes from a young man named Jaydee.

As a young boy, he often spent Sunday mornings with his father at a fishing dock. But unlike everyone else there, they never fished. The first time they went, Jaydee looked around at all the other kids with their fathers as they cast their lines into the water. For hours, he and his father sat there and watched until they left without ever casting a single fishing line.

On the way home, Jaydee was simultaneously sad and angry. He told his father he would never forgive his cruelty for not fishing with him like the other families did. His father looked at him and smiled, saying, "I love you, Jaydee." When the boy didn't respond, his father asked, "Did you notice how happy all the other little boys and girls were? Did you see their smiles? Could you feel the happiness in their hearts?" After a moment of silence Jaydee snapped, "I don't really care! I just want to go fishing like everyone else!"

They went back to the fishing dock dozens of Sunday mornings throughout Jaydee's childhood. Each time they saw little boys and girls jumping and laughing and celebrating as they reeled in fish. But they still never cast a single line into the water. They simply sat there on the end of the dock and watched. Jaydee's father never explained why. But he didn't need to. Because years later as he entered adulthood, Jaydee realized that those mornings he spent sitting on that dock were where he learned how to love.

The Love We Miss

Jaydee's story has truly stayed with us. Too often we compare ourselves to others, and to how we think things "should" be. And we miss what they really are. We miss the love that's right in front of us—coming from the people closest to us as well as those we observe at a distance.

The happiness on display around us is an experience to marvel at and admire. When we take time to do so—to truly witness and listen, instead of bypassing or judging too quickly—we can learn so much . . . about ourselves, about each other, and about love.

5 Character TRAITS
That Make You Happy

WHEN WE LOOK in the mirror, it's often our character (or lack thereof) that speaks the loudest. But not all character traits are created equal, at least not insofar as happiness is concerned. Based on a decade of one-on-one coaching experiences with students and clients, we've found that the following are those traits we are convinced will have the greatest impact on your happiness.

1. Courage

Fear is the great thief of happiness. It sneaks in closed doors and robs us of resolve and the commitment and ability to endure the challenges we face.

Courage, on the other hand, is fear's great nemesis. It allows us to challenge our comfort zones, approach people and situations, embrace life, and accept the pain that's inevitable in all of our lives. Without courage, happiness is little more than an illusion.

2. Patience

Impatience is a major bully to happiness. It pushes happiness out of the neighborhood almost as soon as it shows up.

But learning to accept and allow, to go with the flow and relax a bit, is critical to living a happy life. Impatience is often the irritation we feel at the loss of control. But life bubbles and gurgles in ever-changing and unpredictable ways. It simply is not 100 percent controllable. The more we try to control the outcome of events that boil up around us with any kind of precision, the more frustrated we'll feel.

So breathe. Relax. Take it in. Be patient. Learn to accept uncertainty and buddy up to the unpredictable. Let life happen, at least a little. You'll find it that much more beautiful and joyful when you do.

3. Gratitude

To be grateful is to notice the good amid the bad, the color against the backdrop of gray, the lovely even as it's surrounded by the ugly. It's to count your blessings and recognize how beautiful life is even when life isn't going quite as planned (more on this in the next section).

Learning to be grateful requires seeing what isn't always on the surface. It requires retraining your mind to think about the silver linings in life—letting it permeate your mind-set and the overall way you experience life.

When we're grateful, our problems don't disappear, they simply occupy less space in our hearts, minds, and lives.

4. Love

To recognize the centrality of love to living a happy life, just imagine a life lived without it. Imagine a hateful, loveless life of happiness. Impossible, right? The more love that beats in your heart, the happier and more buoyant your heart will be. The more you love life, the more life will love you back.

Love overlooks weakness and closes its eyes to idiosyncrasies. It accepts, seeks, and empowers what's best in others.

5. Forgiveness

People who hold on to pain, who nurse their wounds, who call out the troops to seek vengeance for the wrongs done to them, may win battles here and there. But the war against unhappiness will largely be lost before it's even started.

Refusal to forgive leads to a self-imposed imprisonment. It's time we freed ourselves by letting old pain dissipate into the darkness, so that new opportunities can take us to greater heights of joy.

So, have you forgiven your parents for their shortcomings? Have you forgiven the playground bully or difficult ex, or your neglectful children, or inconsiderate neighbor? If you haven't, you're picking at the open wounds that can only irritate, infect, and fester.

Instead, open your heart to forgiveness. Then your heart will finally be open enough to catch its share of happiness as well.

6 WAYS to FIND GRATITUDE When Everything Goes Wrong

IN OUR RECENT book, *Getting Back to Happy,* we share this entry from Marc's grandmother's journal, dated 9/16/1977: "Today I'm sitting in my hospital bed waiting to have both my breasts removed. But in a strange way, I feel like the lucky one. Until now I have had no health problems. I'm a sixty-nine-year-old woman in the last room at the end of the hall before the pediatric division of the hospital begins. Over the past few hours I have watched dozens of cancer patients being wheeled by in wheelchairs and rolling beds. None of these patients could be a day older than seventeen."

That journal entry has been hanging up in our home office for the past two decades, and it continues to remind us to practice gratitude through thick and thin. No matter how good or bad we have it on any particular day, we do our best to wake up grateful for our lives, because other people in other places are desperately fighting for theirs.

Think about your own life in this context of gratitude. How often do you let go of what you think your life is supposed to look like, and sincerely appreciate it for everything it is?

If you're anything like the rest of us, it's probably not often enough.

Because finding sincere gratitude is much easier said than done in the hustle of life, especially when hard times hit. The truth is, most of the time we create tragedy in our lives out of fairly minor incidents. Something doesn't go exactly as planned, but rather than learn from the experience, we freak out about it and let stress become us. Or we resist the small bits of progress we've made because we can't achieve exactly what we want all at once.

Here are some ways to find sincere gratitude when everything seems to be going wrong. We're not suggesting we should rejoice at living through disappointing or painful life experiences. But there are ways we can find gratitude as we grow through them, nonetheless.

1. Find gratitude around difficult people.

We expect people to treat us kindly, fairly, and respectfully. But the reality is some people won't. They will lose their tempers or act foolishly, regardless of how we treat them. This must be accepted.

Don't lower your standards, but do remind yourself that removing your expectations of others—especially those who are being difficult—is the best way to avoid being disappointed by them.

When you're forced to deal with a difficult person, you can be grateful for having other people in your life who are far less difficult. You can be grateful for having a way to practice being better at patience, communication, and tempering your expectations. You can think of this person as a teacher who is inadvertently helping you to grow stronger as a person. And, at the very least, you can be grateful for them because they serve as a great reminder of how not to be.

2. Find gratitude when you catch yourself complaining.

Many of us have developed a subtle habit of complaining when things don't go quite our way. Gratitude is the antidote. Each time you notice yourself feeling bitter, or complaining, notice the story in your mind about "how life should be." Instead of letting this story dominate you, find a small way to be grateful instead. What could you feel grateful for right now? What could you appreciate about this moment?

Remember, there's always something to be negative about—and something to be grateful for. The choice is ours.

3. Find gratitude when you are overwhelmed.

Have you ever noticed how the more familiar you become with an amazing situation or relationship in your life, the more you seem to take it for granted—and even feel annoyed or overwhelmed in busy and stressful times? Challenge yourself to flip your perspective in these moments, using a simple reframing tool we call *". . . and I love it!"*

ADD THIS PHRASE to any overwhelming thought:

> *I need to go grocery shopping, and pay the bills, and pick the kids up from school in an hour . . . and I love it!*
>
> *My inbox is filled with two dozen client e-mails that need a response today . . . and I love it!*

Let this little reframing tool give you the perspective you need. Because, again, the everyday things that overwhelm us are often blessings in disguise.

OK, now for some harder stuff . . .

4. Find gratitude after job loss.

No one wins at chess by only moving forward; sometimes you have to move backward to put yourself in a position to win. And that's a good metaphor for your life's work too.

As painful as losing your job is, it's an ending that leads to the beginning of everything that comes next. Let the heaviness of being successful be replaced by the lightness of starting over. This new beginning is the start of a different story, the opportunity to refresh your life, to reinvent who you are.

Remind yourself, as often as necessary, that you can find gratitude for where you are. You can find gratitude for these moments of reinvention—for pushing into the discomfort of getting good at interviewing, learning new skills, and leveling up. You can find gratitude for the opportunity to grow stronger, even in the midst of the growing pains that ultimately get you there.

5. Find gratitude amid health problems.

A couple of years ago, on the second-to-last day of her life, a close friend of ours shared that her only regret was that she didn't appreciate every year with the same passion and purpose that she had in the last two years of her life, after she was diagnosed with terminal cancer. "I've accomplished so much recently, and truly appreciated every step," she said. "If I had only known, I would have started sooner."

Her words made us cry and smile at the same time. What was truly miraculous was seeing the genuine gratitude in her eyes at that moment. And her sentiment has always remained with us. So, while health problems are never fun, the pain can be mediated by a sense of gratitude for having a chance to move forward on our own terms. Of having a life worth living, from moment to precious moment.

6. Find gratitude when someone you love dies.

As we know firsthand, when you lose someone you can't imagine living without, your heart breaks wide open. And the bad news is you never completely get over the loss—you will never forget them. However, we have the ability to push through the experience, and even find meaning in it.

Ultimately, we grew to appreciate that although death is an ending, it is also a necessary part of living. Limits illuminate beauty, and death is the ultimate limit—a reminder that we need to celebrate this beautiful person, and appreciate this beautiful thing called life. Although deeply sad, this passing forces us to gradually reinvent our lives, and in this reinvention is an opportunity to experience beauty in new, unseen ways and places. And finally, death is an opportunity to celebrate a person's life, and to be grateful for the beauty they showed us.

Life's disappointments and struggles are not easy to find gratitude for, but they can become incredible paths of growth if we find the lessons in them—if we start to see everything as our teacher. Truly, the best time to focus on being grateful is when you don't feel like it. Because that's when doing so can make the biggest difference.

10 HABITS You Must QUIT to Be Happy

WHEN YOU QUIT doing the wrong things, you make more room for the things that make you happy. So starting today . . .

1. Quit procrastinating on your goals.

Some people dream of success while others wake up and work hard at it. Action and change are often resisted when they're needed most. The secret to getting ahead is simply getting started. So forget about the finish line and just concentrate on taking your first small, imperfect step.

2. Quit blaming others and making excuses.

Stop blaming others for what you have or don't have, or for what you feel or don't feel. When you blame others for what you're going through, you deny responsibility and perpetuate the problem. Stop giving your power away and start taking responsibility for your life. Blaming is just another sorry excuse, and making excuses changes nothing; you and only you are responsible for the next step you take.

3. Quit trying to avoid change.

If nothing ever changed, there would be no sunrise the next morning. Most of us are comfortable where we are even though the whole universe is constantly changing around us. Learning to accept this is vital to our happiness and success. Because only when we change do we grow, and begin to see a world we never knew was possible. And don't forget—however good or bad a situation is now, it will change. So embrace it and keep moving forward.

4. Quit trying to control the uncontrollable.

Some forces are out of your control, but you can always control how you react. The best thing you can do is let go of what you can't control, and invest your energy in the things you can—like your attitude.

5. Quit talking down to yourself.

One of the major reasons we fail is self-doubt and negative self-talk. Listen to the running script in your mind and replace negative thoughts with positive ones. Over time you will change the trajectory of your life.

6. Quit criticizing others.

The negativity you bleed out toward others will gradually cripple your own happiness. So stop worrying about the flaws you see in everyone else, and focus on yourself. Let the constant growth and improvement in your own life keep you so busy that you have no time left to criticize others.

7. Quit running from your problems and fears.

Trust us, if everyone threw their problems in a pile for you to see, you would probably grab yours back. The best approach is to face them head on, no matter how insurmountable they may seem. Fears, in particular, stop you from taking chances and making decisions. Take them on, one small step at a time. Own them, so they can't own you.

8. Quit living in another time and place.

The past is gone, and the future isn't here yet. No matter how much time we spend thinking and lamenting about either, it doesn't change anything.

One of life's sharpest paradoxes is that our brightest future hinges on our ability to pay attention to what we're doing right now, today. Don't fantasize about being on vacation while at work, and don't worry about the work piling up on your desk when you're on vacation. Live for now. Notice the beauty unfolding around you.

9. Quit trying to be someone you're not.

One of the greatest challenges in life is being yourself in a world that's trying to make you like everyone else. Someone will always be prettier, smarter, and younger, but they will never be you. Be yourself and the right people will love you, and you'll love yourself more too.

10. Quit being ungrateful.

Remember, not all the puzzle pieces of life will seem to fit together at first, but in time you'll realize they do, perfectly. So thank the things that didn't work out, because they just made room for the things that will. And thank the ones who walked away from you, because they just made room for the ones who won't.

No matter how good or bad you have it, wake up each day thankful for your life. Move forward with gratitude.

10 Mistakes UNHAPPY People Make

HAPPINESS IS A choice. There are no excuses for not trying to make the very best out of your life. There are no excuses for living in a way that consistently makes you unhappy. Here are ten unhappiness mistakes to avoid:

1. Thinking you have already missed your chance

Each moment of your life, including this one, is a fresh start. Three little words can release you from your past regrets and guide you forward to a positive new beginning. These words are: *"From now on..."*

2. Using failed relationships as an excuse

Life doesn't always introduce you to the people you *want* to meet. Sometimes life puts you in touch with the people you *need* to meet—to help you, to hurt you, to leave you, to love you, and to gradually strengthen you into the person you were meant to become.

3. Changing who you are to satisfy others

No matter how loud their opinions are, others cannot choose who you are. The question should not be, "Why don't they like me when I'm being me?" It should be, "Why am I wasting my time worrying what they think of me?" If you are not hurting anyone with your actions, keep moving forward with your life. Be happy. Be yourself. If others don't like it, then let them be. Life isn't about pleasing everyone.

4. Putting up with negative people and negative thinking

It's time to walk away from all the drama and the people who create it. Surround yourself with those who make you smile. Love the people who treat you right, and pray for the ones who don't. Forget the negative and focus on the positive. Life is too short to be anything but happy. Making mistakes and falling down is a part of life, but getting back up and moving on is what *living* is all about.

5. Focusing all your attention on another time and place

This day will never happen again. Enjoy it. Cherish your time. It's often hard to tell the true value of a moment until it becomes a memory. Someday you may discover that the small things were really the big things. So learn to appreciate what you have before time forces you to appreciate what you once had.

6. Overlooking what you have, to focus on what you don't

Most people pay more attention to what they're missing, rather than what they have. Instead of thinking about what you're missing, think about what you have that everyone else is missing.

7. Dwelling on the things you can't change

The best often comes after the worst happens. You can either move on, or you can dwell on the things you can't change. Either way, life does move on. So learn from the past and then get the heck out of there. You will always grow stronger from the pain if you don't let it destroy you.

8. Constantly sacrificing your own happiness for everyone else

Never let your own happiness wither away as you try to bring sunshine to others. Life is not about making others happy. Life is about being honest and sharing your happiness with them.

9. Losing track of your own goals and ideals

With all the social conditioning in our society, we sometimes forget to stay true to ourselves. In this crazy world that's trying to make you like everyone else, stay true to your awesome self.

10. Dealing with the stress of deceiving others

If you say you're going to do something, *do it!* If you say you're going to be somewhere, *be there!* If you say you feel something, *mean it!* If you can't, won't, and don't, then say so up front. Live in such a way that if someone decided to attack your character, no one would believe it. Live so that when the people around you think of fairness, caring, and integrity, they think of you.

9 HABITS of Super-POSITIVE People

LIFE IS FULL of positive experiences. Notice them. Live your life to the fullest potential by reveling in the beauty of these experiences, and letting them inspire you to be the most positive version of *you*. Living a positive life is all about creating positive habits to help you focus on what truly matters. This is the secret of super-positive people. Here are nine simple ideas to help you follow in their footsteps:

1. Wake up every morning with the idea that something wonderful is possible today.

Smiling is a healing energy. A consistently positive attitude is the cheapest "fountain of youth." You've got to dance like there's nobody watching, love like you'll never be hurt, sing like there's nobody listening, and live like it's heaven on Earth.

2. Celebrate your existence.

Your mind is the window through which you see the world. The way to make this the happiest day ever is to think, feel, walk, talk, give, and serve like you are the most fortunate person in the whole world. Open-minded, openhearted, and openhanded. Nothing more is needed.

3. Appreciate life's perfect moments.

Your life isn't perfect, but it does have perfect moments. Don't let the little things get you down. Pause to stand in awe of the fact that you have the ability to rediscover life as the miracle it has always been.

4. Embrace life's challenges.

Uncharted territory in your life is not good or bad, it just is. Yes, it may rattle your foundation, and you may be tempted to pull back, say you can't do it, or bail completely. But these are exactly the conditions that set you up for massive amounts of personal growth. Don't run from them—give them the best you've got.

5. Become addicted to constant and never-ending self-improvement.

Every day is a new day to learn, grow, develop your strengths, heal yourself from past regrets, and move forward. It is never too late to switch gears and change things that are not working in your life. Using today wisely will always help you create a more positive tomorrow.

6. Live and breathe the truth.

It's the most positive, stress-free way to live, because the truth always reveals itself eventually anyway. So don't aim to be impressive, aim to be true. That means having integrity—doing the right thing even when you know nobody is watching.

7. Fill your own bucket.

Choose to be happy for no reason at all. Fill your own bucket of happiness so high that the rest of the world can't poke enough holes to drain it dry.

8. Help the people around you smile.

Today, give someone one of your smiles. At the right time, a kind word from a stranger or unexpected encouragement from a friend can make all the difference in the world. Kindness is free, but it's priceless. And as you know, what goes around comes around.

9. Spend time with positive people.

Life's way too awesome to waste time with people who don't treat you right. So surround yourself with people who make you happy and make you smile. People who help you up when you're down. People who would never take advantage of you. People who genuinely care. They are the ones worth keeping in your life. Everyone else is just passing through.

19 Quick Tricks to Feel Better INSTANTLY

WHEN LIFE GETS stressful and you feel like you're losing your emotional balance, use one or more of these simple tricks to help you relax your mind and recenter yourself in an instant:

1. Wash your hands and face, and brush your teeth.
The simple act of cleaning these parts of your body is both reinvigorating and relaxing, and gives you that "fresh start" feeling.

2. Change your socks.
It's an odd trick, but it works. Bring a change of socks to work, and change your socks midway through the day. You'll be amazed at how much fresher you'll feel.

3. Call a close friend.
Sometimes a quick conversation with someone you care about is just what you need to boost your mood.

4. Stretch.

When you feel yourself getting stressed, get up, reach toward the sky, bend down and touch your toes, twist your torso from side to side—stretch it out.

5. Go outdoors.

Getting some fresh air outdoors is always a good way to rouse your senses and clear your mind.

6. Take a light exercise break.

Do a few sets of jumping jacks to get your blood moving, or take a walk. Even the slightest bit of exercise can reduce momentary stress and re-energize your mind.

7. Dress to feel your best.

When we know we are looking our best, we naturally feel better.

8. Listen to your favorite music.

If it's not too much of a distraction, listening to your favorite upbeat music can be a great way to boost your spirits.

9. Take a few deep, controlled breaths.

Deep breathing helps reduce stress, a source of fatigue, and increases the level of oxygen in the blood. Techniques can be as simple as inhaling for five seconds, holding your breath for four seconds, and exhaling for four seconds. You can also try more elaborate techniques that require different positions.

10. Clear your stuffed nose.

If allergies have your sinuses blocked, you may be feeling more tired and negative. Rinse your nasal passages with saline solution.

11. Cook a good meal.

Even if you are by yourself, preparing a tasty dinner, setting the table, and treating yourself to a wonderful culinary experience will lift your spirits. Sharing it with someone you love or respect will make it even more nurturing.

12. Walk away from energy vampires.

Energy vampires are people who always have something to complain about, or a problem that needs to be fixed, and they'll drain your energy by making you listen to them go on and on about their problems or by giving them attention.

13. Complete an important piece of unfinished business.

Today is a perfect day to finish what you started. Few feelings are more satisfying than the one you get after an old burden has been lifted off your shoulders.

14. Work on something that's meaningful to you.

Engage yourself in a personal project. Or pull the trigger on doing something you've wanted to do for a long time, but haven't yet had the resolve to tackle.

15. Assist someone in need.

When you make a positive impact in someone else's life, you also make a positive impact in your own. Do something that helps someone else to be happy or suffer less. We promise, it will be an extremely rewarding experience.

16. Think about your latest (or greatest) success.

Think about it for at least sixty seconds. Taking in your success will help you reach it again and again. Quite simply, it reminds you that if you've done it before, you can do it again.

17. Act like today is already an awesome day.

Research shows that although we think that we act because of the way we feel, in fact, we often feel because of the way we act. A great attitude always leads to great experiences.

18. Notice what's right.

It's easy to overlook what's working. Take a moment to celebrate it—and watch the positive momentum build.

19. Take a moment to acknowledge how far you've come.

We can all lose our feelings of self-worth, especially when something goes wrong. The truth is that if you have done it before, you can do it again, no matter what.

12 Stressful THINGS to STOP Tolerating

YOU CAN'T LIVE a happy, successful, fulfilling life if you're spending all your energy putting up with things that shouldn't be tolerated. Sometimes you need to put your foot down. Here are some things to stop tolerating in your life:

1. The decision to settle for mediocrity

Sometimes growing up means growing apart from old habits, relationships, and situations, and finding something new that truly moves you—something that gets you so excited you can't wait to get out of bed in the morning. That's what life is all about. Don't settle.

2. Your own negative thinking

Your mind is your sacred space. You can close the windows and block the view, or you can open the windows and let light in. It's your choice. The sun is always shining on some part of your life. What do you typically focus on? Sometimes the only thing you need to shift in order to experience more happiness, more love, and more success, is your way of thinking.

3. Other people's negativity

You do not have control over what others say and do, but you can prevent their poisonous words and actions from invading your heart and mind. Remember, if you do not respect your sacred inner space, no one else will either.

4. Unhealthy relationships

Be with people who know your worth. You don't need lots of friends to be happy, just a few real ones who appreciate you for who you are. Often we walk away not because we want others to realize our worth, but because we finally realize our own.

5. Dishonesty

Living a life of honesty creates peace of mind, which is priceless. Don't be dishonest and don't put up with people who are.

6. A work environment or career field you hate

If it doesn't feel right, don't settle on the first or second career track you dabble in. Keep searching. Eventually you will find work you love to do—because hard work isn't hard when you concentrate on your passions.

7. Being disorganized and unprepared

Wake up thirty minutes earlier. That extra time will help you avoid unnecessary headaches. Set yourself up for success.

8. Inaction

You can't change anything or make progress by just sitting back and thinking about it. If you keep doing what you're doing, you'll keep getting what you're getting. The best time to start is now.

9. The lingering of unfinished business

Stop procrastinating. Start taking action to tie up loose ends. Putting something off makes it harder and scarier instantly.

10. The choice to mull over past mistakes and regrets

If you feel like your ship is sinking, this might be a good time to throw out the stuff that's been weighing it down. Let it go. You can't start the next chapter of your life if you keep rereading the previous one.

11. A mounting pile of personal debt

Financial debt causes stress and heartache. Live a comfortable life, not a wasteful one. Do not buy stuff you do not need. Do not spend to impress others. Do not live life trying to fool yourself into thinking wealth is measured in material objects. Manage your money wisely so your money does not manage you.

12. Your reluctance to say what you need to say

No, you shouldn't start shouting obscenities or berating others. But you must say what you need to say, when you need to say it. Don't censor yourself. Speak your truth—with compassion—always.

10 ACTIONS That Always Bring Happiness

HAPPINESS IS NOT something to postpone for the future, it is something you design into the present. Starting today . . .

1. Appreciate what you have.

If we counted our blessings instead of our money, we would all be a lot richer. Happiness is there, wrapped in beauty and hidden delicately between the seconds of your life. If you never stop for a minute to notice, you might miss it.

2. Focus on things that truly matter.

The simple fact that we are even here, alive, on this planet is a wondrous miracle, and we should not spend the time we have being distracted or miserable. Every moment we get is a gift, so stop focusing on unhappy things, and spend your moments on things that truly matter to your heart.

3. Define your own meaning of life, and pursue it.

Don't fear failure, fear a lifetime of mediocrity due to lack of effort and commitment. There are so many people out there who will tell you that you *can't*. Turn around and say, "Watch me!"

4. Embrace life's challenges.

You may think that taking a detour in life is a waste of time and energy, but you can also see the detour as a means of learning more about who you are and where you are heading. Being off the beaten path may be disorienting and confusing at times, yet it challenges your creative spirit to discover new ways to build a stronger *you*.

5. Find the balance that allows you to be who you truly are.

Sometimes you have to step outside of the person you've been and remember the person you were meant to be, the person you are capable of being, and the person you truly are.

6. Love your body enough to take care of it.

Never be ashamed of yourself because you are born into one skin. You can scar it, stretch it, burn it, mark it, tan it, and peel it. But you are always in it, so take care of it and learn to love it.

7. Limit your time with negative people.

Create an environment that helps you make positive choices for the rest of your life. Protect your spirit and potential by limiting your time with negative people.

8. Treat others the way you want to be treated.

Be conscious of your attitude and your actions. You have all the tools at your disposal to do and say whatever you want. But remember, life is a circle—what goes around comes around eventually.

9. Set a good example.

If you want to empower others in your life, you first need to start living the most empowered version of yourself. Believe in what you want so much that it has no choice but to become your reality. And don't ever compare yourself to anyone else; stay focused on your own journey and leave footprints behind.

10. Accept what is, and live for the possibilities that lie ahead.

Never waste your time wondering about what might have been. Get busy thinking about what still might be, and working to make it happen.

HAPPINESS QUESTIONS
TO MAKE YOU THINK

HAPPINESS is a _____ ?

What would make you SMILE right *now*?

What do you do when NOTHING else seems to make you *happy*?

If HAPPINESS was the national currency, what kind of work would make you *rich*?

What is your HAPPIEST childhood memory? What makes it so *special*?

What do you APPRECIATE most about your *current* situation?

What's one BAD habit that makes you *miserable*?

How OLD would you be if you didn't know how *old* you are?

Do you CELEBRATE the *things* you do have?

What MAKES you *smile*?

PART TWO

Adversity

*A smile doesn't always mean a person is happy.
Sometimes it simply means they are strong enough
to face their problems.*

WHEN OUR STORIES HOLD US BACK

SHE RARELY MAKES eye contact. Instead, she looks down at the ground. Because the ground is safer. Because unlike people, it expects nothing in return. The ground just accepts her for who she is.

As she sits at the bar next to me, she stares down at her vodka tonic, and then the ground, and then her vodka tonic. "Most people don't get me," she says. "They ask me questions like, 'What's your problem?' or 'Were you mistreated as a child?' But I never respond. Because I don't feel like explaining myself. And I don't think they really care anyway."

The music is getting loud and I can see that she needs to talk. I ask, "Want to get some fresh air?"

In the chilly night air, she tells me her story. As she speaks, her emotional gaze shifts from the ground, to my eyes, to the moonlit sky, to the ground, and back to my eyes again.

When she finishes, she says, "Well, now you know my story. You think I'm a freak, don't you?"

"Place your right hand on your chest," I tell her. She does. "Do you feel something?" I ask.

"Yeah, I feel my heartbeat."

"Now, place both of your hands on your face and move them around slowly." She does. "What do you feel now?" I ask.

"Well, I feel my eyes, my nose, my mouth . . . I feel my face."

"That's right," I reply. "But unlike you, stories don't have heartbeats, and they don't have faces. Because stories are not alive . . . they're not people. They're just stories."

She stares into my eyes for a long moment, smiles, and says, "Just stories we live through."

"Yeah . . . and stories we learn from."

12 THINGS to Know BEFORE Letting Go

OFTEN, LETTING GO has nothing to do with weakness, and everything to do with strength. And that's what this list is all about—realizing your worth, and identifying the negative ideas, habits, and people in your life that you need to let go of to move forward.

1. The past can steal your present if you let it.

You can spend hours, days, weeks, months, or even years overanalyzing a situation from the past, trying to put the pieces together, justifying what could've or should've happened. Or you can just leave the pieces on the floor and walk out the door into the sunlight.

2. Not everyone, and not everything, is meant to stay.

Some circumstances and people come into our lives just to strengthen us or teach us, so that we can move on without them.

3. Happiness is not the absence of problems, but the ability to deal with them.

Imagine all the wondrous things your mind might embrace if it weren't wrapped so tightly around your struggles. Because it's not what the world takes away from you that counts, it's what you do with what you have left.

4. Sometimes you just need to do your best and surrender the rest.

Tell yourself, "I am doing the best I can with what I have in this moment. And that is all I can expect of anyone, including me." Love yourself and be proud of everything you do, even your mistakes. Because even mistakes mean you're trying.

5. You are in control of only one person: yourself.

Letting go in your relationships doesn't always mean that you don't care about others anymore; it's simply realizing that the only person you really have control over is yourself.

6. What's right for you may be wrong for others, and vice versa.

Think for yourself, and allow others the privilege of doing so too. You need to live your life your way—the way that's right for you.

7. Some people will refuse to accept you for who you are.

When you're comfortable in your skin, not everyone will like you, and that's OK. It's always worth doing what's right and being true to yourself.

8. Relationships can only exist on a steady foundation of truth.

When you build relationships based on truth and authenticity, rather than masks, false perfection, and being phony, your relationships will heal, connect, and thrive.

9. The world changes when you change.

Our thoughts and perceptions create our world. If you truly want to change your life, you must first change your mind.

10. You can make decisions, or you can make excuses.

Don't let what you *can't* do stop you from what you *can*. Do what you can with what you have right now. Stop overthinking and start *doing!*

11. It usually takes just a few negative remarks to kill a person's dream.

Don't kill people's dreams with negative words, and don't put up with those who do. Don't let people interrupt you and tell you that you can't do something. If you have a dream that you're passionate about, you must protect it, and help others do the same.

12. Sometimes walking away is the only way to win.

Never waste your time trying to explain yourself to people who have shown they don't care. In other words, don't define your intelligence by the number of arguments you have won, but by the number of times you have said, "This needless nonsense is not worth my time."

10 THINGS You Must GIVE UP to Move Forward

IF YOU WANT to move on to better things, you have to give up what's weighing you down—which is not always as obvious and easy as it sounds. Starting today, give up . . .

1. Letting the opinions of others control your life

In the end, it's not what others think, it's what you think about yourself that counts. Sometimes you have to do exactly what's best for you and your life, not what's best for everyone else.

2. The shame of past failures

Your past does not equal your future. Just because you failed yesterday, or today, or for the last six months, or the last sixteen years, doesn't have any impact on the current moment. All that matters is what you do right now.

3. Being indecisive about what you want

When you're passionate, you're energized. Likewise, when you lack passion, your energy is low and unproductive. Make a decision to figure out what you want, and then pursue it passionately.

4. Procrastinating on the goals that matter to you

We have two primary choices in life: to accept conditions as they exist, or accept the responsibility for changing them. Don't give up trying to do what you really want to do. When there is love and inspiration, you can't go wrong. A year from now, you will wish you had started today.

5. Choosing to do nothing

Every day is a new chance to choose. Choose to shift your perspective. Choose to turn on the light and stop fretting about insecurity and doubt. Choose to do work that you are proud of. Choose to truly *live*, right now.

6. Your need to be right

Aim for success, but never give up your right to be wrong. Because when you do, you will also lose your ability to learn new things and move forward with your life.

7. Running from problems that should be fixed

We make life harder than it has to be. The difficulties started when . . . conversations became texting, feelings became subliminal, sex became a game, the word "love" fell out of context, trust faded as honesty waned, jealously became a habit, being hurt started to feel natural, and running away from it all became our solution. Face these issues, fix the problems, communicate, appreciate, forgive, and *love* the people in your life who deserve it.

8. Making excuses rather than decisions

Life is a continuous exercise in creative problem solving. A mistake doesn't become a failure until you refuse to correct it. Thus, most long-term failures are the outcome of people who make excuses instead of decisions.

9. Overlooking the positive points in your life

What we see often depends entirely on what we're looking for. Do your best and surrender the rest. When you stay stuck in regret over the life you think you should have had, you end up missing the beauty of what you do have. Start being thankful for the good things in your life right now.

10. Not appreciating the present moment

We do not remember days, we remember moments. Too often we try to accomplish something big without realizing that the greatest part of life is made up of the little things. Live authentically and cherish each precious moment of your journey.

3 HARD Questions:
The TRIPLE-FILTER Test

A COUPLE THOUSAND years ago in ancient Greece, the great philosopher Socrates was strolling contemplatively around a town square when a neighbor walked up to him and said, "You're never in a million years going to believe what I just heard about our mutual friend—"

"Wait," Socrates interrupted, putting his hand up in the air. "Before you continue with this story, your words must pass the triple-filter test."

"The what?"

"The triple-filter test," Socrates said.

The neighbor just stared at him with a blank expression.

Socrates continued, "The first filter is *Truth*. Are you absolutely sure the story you are about to tell me is true?"

"Well, no," the neighbor said, "I literally just heard it from someone else I know."

"Aha . . ." Socrates quickly replied. "Then let's move on to the second filter. Is what you are about to share *Good* in any way, shape, or form?"

"No . . . no," the neighbor said, "this story is actually quite—"

Before he could finish his sentence, Socrates interrupted him again. "Ahh . . . so it may not be true and it is definitely not good."

"That's right," the neighbor assured him.

"Well, you may still be able to save yourself," Socrates said. "Is anything about the story you want to share *Useful*?"

The neighbor stared blankly again for a moment and then said, "No, I suppose it's not really—"

"So, you want to tell me something that may not be true, is definitely not good, and is not useful to know?" Socrates asked. The neighbor looked down at the ground and nodded. "Well, you have no good reason to tell me this story, and you have no good reason to believe it yourself," Socrates added as the neighbor dolefully walked away.

In many ways, not too much has changed since ancient Greece, especially when it comes to the stories we tell ourselves and each other. Every single day, we invest valuable time and energy in drama and hearsay. Many of us plug into social media first thing in the morning for reasons that have zero to do with what is true for us, good for us, and useful for those around us. Instead, we do it mostly just to distract ourselves . . . from ourselves.

In an expansive universe in which there are abundant opportunities to discover what's true, what's good, and what's useful, when we do the opposite, we know it. And while making that compromise—with lots of mind-numbing distractions—is tolerable for a little while, eventually it isn't anymore. Our negligence catches up to us, and we begin to feel pain.

Then, on really hard days, when the drama and hearsay just aren't enough to distract us from the pain that's been gradually building up in our minds, we begin to feel utterly broken inside.

Don't fall into the trap of breaking yourself down like that for no reason. Instead, take Socrates's advice: simply focus on what is true, good, and useful. It worked well for Socrates a couple thousand years ago, and we assure you it continues to work well for many people today.

16 HARSH TRUTHS
That Make Us Stronger

1. Life is not easy.

Hard work makes people lucky—it's the stuff that brings dreams to reality. So start every morning ready to run farther than you did yesterday and fight harder than you ever have before.

2. You will fail sometimes.

The faster you accept this, the faster you can get on with moving forward. So don't let failure get to your heart (or success get to your head). Do your best and let your consistent daily actions speak for themselves over the long term.

3. Right now, there's a lot you don't know.

The day you stop learning is the day you stop living. Embrace new information, think about it, and use it to advance yourself.

4. There may not be a tomorrow.

Not for everyone. This is sad but true. So spend your time wisely today and pause long enough to appreciate it.

5. There's a lot you can't control.

You don't have to control everything to find peace and happiness. It lives with you always, deep within. See what happens when you loosen your grip, throw your hands into the air, and allow life to just happen and flow.

6. Information is not true knowledge.

Knowledge comes from experience. You can discuss a task a hundred times, but these discussions will only give you a philosophical understanding. You must tackle a task firsthand to truly understand it.

7. You can't be successful without providing value.

Don't waste your time trying to be successful. Spend your time adding value to the world around you.

8. Someone else will always have more than you.

Whether it's money, friends, or magic beans, there will always be someone who has more than you. But remember, it's not how many you have, it's how passionate you are about collecting them. It's all about the journey.

9. You can't change the past.

You can't change what happened, but you can change how you react to it.

10. The only person who can make you happy is you.

The root of your happiness comes from your relationship with yourself. Sure, external entities can have fleeting effects on your mood, but in the long run nothing matters more than how you feel about who you are on the inside.

11. There will always be people who don't like you.

You can't be everything to everyone. So concentrate on doing what you know in your heart is right. What others think and say about you isn't all that important. What's essential is how you feel about yourself.

12. You won't always get what you want.

To paraphrase Mick Jagger, you won't always get what you want, but if you try sometimes, you might get what you need. Look around. Appreciate the things you have right now.

13. In life, you get what you put in.

If you want love, give love. If you want friends, be one. If you want money, provide value.

14. Some friends will come and go.

Many of your friends from one chapter of your life won't be there for future chapters. But some friends will stick. And it's these friends—the ones who transcend time and circumstance—who matter.

15. Doing the same exact thing every day hinders self-growth.

If you keep doing what you're doing, you'll keep getting what you're getting. Growth happens when you change things—when you try new things and stretch beyond your comfort zone.

16. You will never feel 100 percent ready for something new.

Because most great opportunities in life force us to grow beyond our comfort zone, you won't feel totally comfortable or ready for change when you're faced with it. Don't run from it—go for it instead.

12 WAYS to Get a SECOND CHANCE in Life

WE ALL NEED second chances. This isn't a perfect world. We're probably on our one thousandth second chance right now and we are not ashamed to admit it. Because even though we have failed a lot, it means we have tried a lot too.

The only difference between an opportunity and an obstacle is attitude. Getting a second chance in life is about giving yourself the opportunity to grow beyond your past failures. Here's how:

1. Let go of the past.

Every difficult moment in our lives is accompanied by an opportunity for personal growth and creativity. But in order to attain this growth and creativity, we must first learn to let go of the past. We must recognize that difficulties pass like everything else in life. And once they pass, all we're left with are our unique experiences and the lessons required to make a better attempt next time.

2. Identify the lesson.

Everything is a life lesson. Everyone you meet, everything you encounter. Never forget to acknowledge the lesson, especially when things don't go your way. If you don't get a job you wanted or a relationship doesn't work, something better is out there waiting. And the lesson you just learned is the first step toward it.

3. Lose the negative attitude.

Negative thinking creates negative results. Positive thinking creates positive results. Every one of the suggestions in this book is irrelevant if your mind is stuck in the gutter. Positive thinking is at the heart of every great success story. The mind must believe it can do something before it is capable of actually doing it.

4. Accept accountability for your current situation.

You are the only one who can directly control the outcome of your life. And no, it won't always be easy. Everyone faces a maze of obstacles. You must accept accountability for your situation and overcome the obstacles. Choosing not to is giving up on the life you were meant to create.

5. Focus on the things you can change.

Some forces are out of your control. Do the best you can with the resources you have. Wasting your time, talent, and emotional energy on things that are beyond your control is a recipe for frustration, misery, and stagnation. Invest your energy in the things you can change.

6. Figure out what you really want.

You'll be running on a hamster wheel forever if you never decide where you want to go. Some of us were born to be musicians, or poets, or entrepreneurs. Don't quit just because you didn't get it right on your first shot. And don't waste your life fulfilling someone else's dreams and desires. Follow your intuition and make a decision to never give up on who you are capable of becoming.

7. Eliminate the nonessential.

First, identify the essential—the things in your life that matter most to you. Then eliminate the fluff. This drastically simplifies things and leaves you with a clean slate—a fresh, solid foundation to build upon without needless interference. This process works with any aspect of your life—work projects, relationships, general to-do lists, and more.

Remember, you can't accomplish anything if you're trying to accomplish everything. Concentrate on the essential. Get rid of the rest.

8. Be specific.

When you set new goals for yourself, try to be as specific as possible. "I want to lose twenty pounds" is a goal you can aim to achieve. "I want to lose weight" is not. And be specific with your actions too. "I will exercise" is too vague to be actionable. "I will take a thirty-minute jog every weekday at six p.m." is something you can actually do—something you can build a routine around—and something you can measure.

9. Concentrate on doing instead of not doing.

"Don't think about eating that chocolate donut!" What are you thinking about now? Eating that chocolate donut, right? Instead of concentrating on eliminating bad habits, concentrate on creating good ones (that just happen to replace the bad ones). Soon you'll start doing the right thing without even thinking about it.

10. Create a daily routine.

It's so simple, but creating a daily routine for yourself can change your life. The most productive routines, we've found, come at the start and end of the day. That means develop a routine for when you wake up, for when you first start working, for when you finish your work, and for the hour or two before you go to sleep. Doing so will help you focus on the important stuff, instead of the distractions that keep popping up. And most important, it will help you make steady progress—which is what second chances are all about.

11. Maintain self-control and work on it for real.

If you want a real second chance, you've got to be willing to give it all you've got. This means you have to strengthen and maintain your self-control. Start with just one activity and make a plan for how you will deal with troubles when they arise. For instance, if you're trying to lose weight, come up with a list of healthful snacks you can eat when you get the craving for snacks. It will be hard in the beginning, but it will get easier. And that's the whole point. As your strength grows, you can take on bigger challenges.

12. Forget about impressing people.

So many people buy things they don't need with money they don't have to impress people they don't know. Don't be one of these people. Just keep doing what you know is right. And if you don't reach your goal, adjust your approach and try again. You'll get there eventually.

12 TOUGH TRUTHS That Help You Grow

YOU CAN'T CONTROL everything. Sometimes you just need to relax and have faith that things will work out. Let go a little and let life happen. Because sometimes the truths you can't change end up changing you and helping you grow. Here are twelve such truths:

1. Everything is as it should be.

It's crazy how you always end up where you're meant to be—how even the most tragic and stressful situations eventually teach you important lessons that you never dreamed you were going to learn. Remember, often when things are falling apart, they are actually falling into place.

2. Often it's not until you are lost that you can begin to find your true self.

Making a big life change is pretty scary. But you know what's even scarier? Regret. Vision without action is a daydream, and action without vision is a nightmare. Your heart is free; have the courage to follow it.

3. It's usually the deepest pain that empowers you to grow to your full potential.

It's often the scary, stressful choices that end up being the most worthwhile. Without pain, there would be no change. But remember that pain, just like everything in life, is meant to be learned from and then released.

4. One of the hardest decisions you will ever face in life is choosing to walk away.

If you catch yourself in a cycle of trying to change someone, or defending yourself against someone who is trying to change you, walk away. But if you are pursuing a dream, take another step. And don't forget that sometimes this step will involve modifying your dream or planning a new one—it's OK to change your mind or have more than one dream.

5. You have to take care of yourself first.

Before supporting others, you have to support yourself. Before correcting others, you have to correct yourself. Before making others happy, you have to make yourself happy. It's not selfishness, it's personal development. Once you balance yourself, you can begin to balance the world around you.

6. One of the greatest freedoms is truly not caring what everyone else thinks of you.

As long as you are worried about what others think of you, you are owned by them. Only when you require no approval from outside yourself can you own yourself.

7. You may need to be single for a while.

Owning your issues—and facing them—will make you far happier, in the long run, than repeating them again and again and expecting a different result.

8. The only thing you can absolutely control is how you react to things out of your control.

The more you can adapt to the situations in life, the more powerful your highs will be, and the more quickly you'll be able to bounce back from the lows. Put most simply: Being at peace means being in a state of complete acceptance of all that is, right here, right now.

9. Some people will lie to you.

Pay less attention to what people say, and more attention to what they do. Their actions will show you the truth, which will help you measure the true quality of your relationship in the long term.

10. If you concentrate on what you don't have, you will never have enough.

Abundance is not about how much you have, it's how you feel about what you have. When you take things for granted, your happiness fades away.

11. Yes, you have failed in the past.

Just because you're not where you want to be today doesn't mean you won't be there someday. You can turn it all around by making a simple choice to stand back up—to try again, to love again, to live again, and to dream again.

12. Everything is going to be all right—maybe not today, but eventually.

There will be times when it seems like everything that could possibly go wrong does. And you might feel like you will be stuck in this rut forever, but you won't. Sometimes it's just a matter of us staying as positive as possible until the sunshine breaks through the clouds again.

30 LESSONS for FINDING Strength in Hard Times

NOBODY GETS THROUGH life without losing someone they love, someone they need, or something they thought was meant to be. But it is these losses that make us stronger and eventually move us toward future opportunities for growth and happiness.

Over the past decade, we've had our share of painful losses. When our time of mourning was over in each circumstance, we pressed forward, stronger and with a greater understanding and respect for life. Here are some lessons we've learned along the way:

1. You are not what happened to you in the past.

No matter how chaotic the past has been, the future is a clean, fresh, wide-open slate. You are not your past habits or failures. You are not how others have at one time treated you. You are only who you think you are right now in this moment. You are only what you do right now in this moment.

2. Focus on what you have, not on what you don't.

The important thing is simply to find one *positive* thought that inspires and helps you move forward. Hold on to it tight, and focus on it. Let it inspire you to start moving forward again.

3. Struggling with problems is a natural part of growing.

Part of growing up is experiencing unexpected troubles in life. People lose jobs, get sick, and sometimes die in car accidents. The smartest, and oftentimes hardest, thing we can do in these kinds of situations is to be tempered in our reactions. And to remember that tragedies are rarely as bad as they seem, and even when they are, they give us an opportunity to grow stronger.

4. It's OK to fall apart for a little while.

You don't always have to pretend to be strong, and there is no need to constantly try to prove that everything is going well. Cry if you need to—it's healthy to shed your tears. The sooner you do, the sooner you will be able to smile again, and face your problems head-on.

5. Life is fragile, sudden, and shorter than it often seems.

Spend your time wisely today and pause long enough to appreciate it. Every moment you get is a gift. Don't waste time by dwelling on the past. Spend it on things that move you in the direction you want to go.

6. Emotionally separate yourself from your problems.

You are far greater than your problems. You are a living, breathing human being who is infinitely more complex than all of your individual problems added up together. And that means you're more powerful than them—you have the ability to change them, and to change the way you feel about them.

7. Don't make a problem bigger than it is.

You should never let one dark cloud cover the entire sky. The sun is always shining on some part of your life. Sometimes you just have to forget how you feel, remember what you deserve, and keep pushing forward.

8. View every challenge as an educational assignment.

Ask yourself: "What is this situation meant to teach me?" Every situation in our lives has a lesson to teach us. Some of these lessons include: To become stronger. To communicate more clearly. To trust your instincts. To express your love. To forgive. To know when to let go. To try something new.

9. Things change, but the sun always rises the next day.

The bad news: nothing is permanent. The good news: nothing is permanent.

10. Giving up and moving on are two very different things.

There comes a point when you get tired of chasing everyone and trying to fix everything, but it's not giving up, and it's not the end. It's a new beginning. It's realizing, finally, that you don't need certain people and things and the drama they bring.

11. Perfect relationships don't exist.

There's no such thing as a perfect, ideal relationship. It's how two people deal with the imperfections of a relationship that makes it ideal.

12. You must love yourself too.

There's nothing selfish about self-care and self-love. We can't give what we don't have. Enrich your life and you'll be life-giving to others. Your contribution to the world matters, but you can only transmit genuine positive energy when you're in a positive place yourself.

13. Don't let others make decisions for you.

Sometimes you just have to live not caring what they think of you, shake off the drama, and prove to *yourself* that you're better than they think you are.

14. Resentment hurts you, not them.

Always forgive people and move on, even if they never ask for your forgiveness. Don't do it for them, do it for you. Grudges are a waste of happiness. Get that unnecessary stress out of your life right now.

15. Consciously nurture your inner hope.

A loss, a worry, an illness, a dream crushed—no matter how deep your hurt or how high your aspirations, do yourself a favor and pause at least once a day, place your hands over your heart, and say aloud, "Hope lives here."

16. It's better to be hurt by the truth than comforted by a lie.

You must see things how they are instead of how you hoped, wished, or expected them to be. It's always better to be slapped with the truth than kissed with a lie.

17. Not getting what you want can be a blessing.

Not getting what you want is sometimes a wonderful stroke of good luck, because it forces you to reevaluate things, opening new doors to opportunities and information you would have otherwise over-looked.

18. Laughter is the best medicine for stress.

Laugh at yourself often. Find the humor in whatever situation you're in. Optimism is a happiness magnet. If you stay positive, good things and good people will be drawn to you.

19. Worrying is literally a waste of energy.

Worry will not drain tomorrow of its troubles, it will drain you of your strength today.

20. Even when it's hard to move, take small steps forward.

Especially in trying times, it's important to continuously push yourself forward. Because momentum is everything! As long as you keep the momentum positive—even if you're moving at a snail's pace—you'll eventually get to the finish line. So celebrate every step you take today, no matter how small. Every step will lead you farther away from where you were yesterday and closer to where you want to be tomorrow.

21. You are better off without some people you thought you needed.

The sad truth is, there are some people who will only be there for you as long as you have something they need. When you no longer serve a purpose for them, they will leave. The good news is, if you tough it out, you'll eventually weed these people out of your life and be left with some great friends you can always count on.

22. You are only competing against yourself.

When you catch yourself comparing yourself to a colleague, neighbor, friend, or someone famous, stop! Realize that you are different, with different strengths—strengths these other people don't possess. Take a moment to reflect on all the awesome abilities you have and to be grateful for all the good things in your life.

23. Life is not easy.

If you expect it to be, you will perpetually disappoint yourself. Achieving anything worthwhile in life takes effort. So start every morning ready to run farther than you did yesterday and fight harder than you ever have before. Above all, make sure you properly align your efforts with your goals. It won't be easy, but it will be worth it in the end.

24. Your future is unwritten.

Regardless of how filthy your past has been, your future is still spotless. Don't start your day with the broken pieces of yesterday. Each day is a new beginning. Every morning we wake up is the first day of the rest of our life. One of the very best ways to get beyond past troubles is to concentrate all of your attention and effort on doing something that your future self will thank you for.

25. You are not trapped, you just need to relearn a few things.

We all have doubts that make us feel trapped at times. If you doubt your ability to make a life-altering decision, to take on a new chapter in your life, or to fend for yourself after years of being overly fostered, consider this: Surely if a bird with healthy wings is locked in a cage long enough, she will doubt her own ability to fly. You still have your wings, but your muscles are weak. Train them and stretch them slowly. Give yourself time. You'll be flying again soon.

26. Everything in life is two-sided.

There is good reason why we can't expect to feel pleasure without ever feeling pain; joy without ever feeling sorrow; confident without ever feeling fear; calm without ever feeling restless; hope without ever feeling despair: there is no such thing as a one-sided coin in life, with which one can buy a pain-free, trouble-free existence.

27. You always have a choice.

No matter what, there are always at least two options. If you can't physically change something, you can change the way you think about it. You can view a crisis as an invitation to learn something new, viewing the shake-up in your outer world as an enlightening opportunity to wake up your inner world.

28. Let others in when you're in a dark place.

No, they won't always be able to pull you out of the dark place you're in, but the light that spills in when they enter will at least show you which way the door is.

29. If you ask negative questions, you will get negative answers.

There are no positive answers to "Why me?," "Why didn't I?," "What if?," and so on. Would you allow someone else to ask you the demoralizing questions you sometimes ask yourself? I doubt it. So stop, and swap them for questions that push you in a positive direction. For instance, "What have I learned from this experience?," "What do I have control over?," "What can I do right now to move forward?"

30. The end is a new beginning.

Say to yourself: "Dear Past, thank you for all the life lessons you have taught me. Dear Future, I am ready now!" Because a great beginning always occurs at the point you thought would be the end of everything.

12 Happy Thoughts for TROUBLED Times

PEOPLE AND CIRCUMSTANCES will occasionally break you down. But if you keep your mind focused, your heart open to possibility, and continue to put one foot in front of the other, you will be able to quickly recover the pieces, rebuild, and come back much stronger than you ever would have been otherwise. Here are a few happy thoughts to ponder on those days when the whole world seems like it's crashing down around you:

1. Down days are completely normal and not something you should feel guilty about having.

Happiness is never constant. Surrendering to your sadness, or whatever negative emotion is trying to come to the surface, does not make you a bad person. But remember, if you aren't sincerely thankful for every smile, don't be totally shocked by every tear. Keep things in perspective.

2. When you are at your lowest point, you are open to the greatest positive change.

Happiness is not the absence of problems, it's the strength to deal with them. Strength doesn't come from what you can do, it comes from overcoming the things you once thought you couldn't do.

3. There is a huge difference between giving up and moving on.

Moving on doesn't mean giving up, but rather accepting that there are some things that cannot be. Moving on can mean that you're making a choice to be happy rather than hurt. For some folks, good situations last a lifetime, but for many, not knowing when to move on can hold them back forever.

4. Life rarely turns out exactly the way you want it to, but you still have an opportunity to make it great.

You have to do what you can, with what you have, exactly where you are. It won't always be easy, but it will be worth it in the end. Remember that there is no perfect life, just perfect moments. And it's these moments you must cherish; it's these moments that make the whole journey worthwhile.

5. Long-term happiness can only be felt if you don't set conditions.

Accept life unconditionally. Realize that life balances itself between the ideal and the disappointing. And the disappointments are just life's way of saying, "I've got something better for you right around the corner." So be patient, live life, accept what is, and have a little faith.

6. Too often, we carry around things from our past that hurt us.

Don't let regrets, shame, pain, and anger from the past rob you of your present happiness. Let go, move on, and walk forward.

7. You can choose to view things differently.

Pick one part of your life that you are unhappy with and look at it from a different point of view. See the rain as nourishment for future growth. Consider being alone for a while to create the solitude you need to hear your inner voice. Right now, you can choose to allow the light to shine in your life. Why not allow it?

8. Stand strong.

Whatever life throws at you, even if it hurts, fight through it. Remember, strong walls shake but never collapse. Life always offers you another chance—if you're willing to take it.

9. When your flaws are stitched together with good intentions, your flaws make you beautiful.

Never apologize for what makes you *you*. Never let someone else tell you who you are. Accept no one's definition of your life except your own.

10. You have the ability to heal yourself.

Just like lava flowing slowly out of a volcano, you must create a healthy outlet for your pain and anger. It's important after you've been hurt to take some time to think about your pain, and address it calmly and consciously, so you can thwart the possibility of more pain brewing from your own negativity.

11. There's a lot of life left to be lived.

The real tragedy in life is not death, but the passion we let die inside of us while we still live. Remember, troubles from the past cannot define you, destroy you, or defeat you all by themselves. As long as you keep pushing forward, they can only strengthen you.

12. You are a work in progress.

Today is a fresh start. Replace negativity with positivity. Inspire yourself. Give someone a compliment. Take a chance on an idea you believe in. You have the opportunity to do these things every single day—to make the necessary changes and slowly become the person you want to be. You just have to decide to do it. Decide that today is the day. Say it: "This is going to be my day!"

WHAT YOU NEED TO KNOW WHEN TRAGEDY STRIKES

The Accident

Tragedy strikes a man who isn't yet old. A minivan traveling toward him on a dark mountain highway hits his car nearly head-on just after sunset. He grasps his steering wheel hard and veers into the rocky mountainside until his car screeches to a halt. The minivan flips onto its side and skids in the other direction off the cliff, plummeting five hundred feet to the ground. Inside is a young family of five.

He doesn't recall the events that followed during the next few days. He doesn't recall the three eyewitnesses who comforted him and assured him that it wasn't his fault—that the other driver had swerved into his lane. He doesn't recall how he got to the emergency room or the fact that he stayed there for five days to treat a concussion and a broken collarbone.

The Guilt

What he does know—and clearly recalls—are the endless string of days he passes sitting alone in his bedroom, crying, and thinking, "Why me?" Why, after forty-eight years of Sunday church attendance, unwavering faith, and regular community volunteering and charity, would God ask him to spend the rest of his life knowing that he single-handedly killed an entire family?

He has a loving, supportive family that tries to comfort his ailing heart, but he can only see them as the loving family he has taken from the world. He also has an overflowing network of close friends who want to see him smile again, but they now represent friends that others have lost because of him.

The man who isn't yet old begins to age more rapidly. Within a few short months, he is a shell of his former self—skin and bones, wrinkles creasing his face, a despondent downward gaze, and a hole in his heart that has grown so wide he feels like there's nothing left at all.

All of the people around him—those family members and friends who care so much—have done everything in their power to revive him to his former self. When love didn't work, they tried relaxing vacations. When vacations didn't work, they tried getting him involved in community activities. When the community activities didn't work, they tried doctors. And now they have resigned from trying. Because the man who is now an old man has completely resigned from everything.

The Dream

A night comes when he decides that it's just not worth it anymore—that it's time to leave this world behind. Perhaps to go somewhere better. Perhaps to go nowhere at all. Luckily, he decides to sleep on it, because he barely has the strength to keep his eyelids open. So he closes his eyes and instantly falls into a deep sleep.

And he begins to dream. In the dream, he is sitting in a dimly lit room at a round table across from an elderly woman who looks much like his late mother. They stare at each other in silence for several minutes and then the elderly woman speaks.

"My son, tragedy is simply a miracle waiting to be discovered. Because within tragedy lie the seeds of love, learning, forgiveness, and empathy. If we choose to plant these seeds, they grow strong. If, on the other hand, we choose to overlook them, we prolong our tragedy and let somebody else discover the miracle."

The old man cries in his dream and in his sleep. He thinks about his wife, and his children, and all of the wonderful people who care for him. And he suddenly realizes that instead of using the tragic accident to notice how precious life is, he has prolonged the tragedy and essentially ceased to live his life. And he is very close, now, to passing all of his pain and sorrow over to the people he loves most in this world.

A New Beginning

He opens his eyes and takes a deep breath. He is alive. He realizes that he still has an opportunity to change things . . . To mend the broken pieces and experience the miracle that comes after the tragedy . . . To plant the seeds of love, learning, forgiveness, and empathy, and water these seeds until they grow strong.

He rolls over and kisses his wife on the cheek and ruffles her hair until her eyelids begin to flutter. She opens her eyes and looks at him, totally confused. There's a spark in his eyes that she hasn't seen in a long while—a spark that she thought had died with his youth on the day of the accident. "I love you so much," he says. "I've missed you," she replies. "Welcome back."

ADVERSITY QUESTIONS
TO MAKE YOU THINK

What STANDS between *you* and *happiness?*

Decisions are being made right now. The question is are you MAKING them *yourself* or are you letting others make them for you?

What is the biggest CHALLENGE you face *right now?*

What's SOMETHING bad that happened to you that made you *stronger?*

Are you AWARE that *someone* has it *worse* than you?

Are you holding on to SOMETHING you need to *let go?*

Do you REMEMBER that time five years ago when you were extremely upset? Does it really *matter now?*

If the average human life span was forty years, how would you LIVE your life *differently?*

What is WORTH the *pain?*

What's MISSING in your *life?*

PART THREE

· · · · ·

Relationships

*In life you'll realize there is a purpose for everyone
you meet. Some will test you, some will use you,
and some will teach you. But most important,
some will bring out the best in you.*

WHO WILL SAVE YOUR LIFE?

IN THE SUMMER of 1997, at the age of fifteen, I learned a valuable life lesson. And I learned it the hard way.

Leave It There for Now

"Go deep!" Roger shouts. I sprint as fast as I can, but not fast enough. The football flies over my head, bounces off the ground, and takes a massive leap over the schoolyard's fence. It lands in private property on the opposite side.

"Ahh ... jeez!" I yelp. "That's the witch lady's yard! You're going to go get that!"

"No, I'm not!" Roger insists. "I had to deal with that freak last week. So this time it's your turn."

"Man, she creeps me out! The way she speaks ... and that hairy mole on her nose ... yuck! I don't feel like dealing with her. I'd rather just leave my football there for now and get it later."

"Fair enough, I'm ready to do something else anyway," Roger replies. "Let's head over to the arcade. I wouldn't mind whupping your butt in a few rounds of *Street Fighter*."

We jump on our bikes and pedal off to the arcade.

It's Too Late

Thirty minutes later, we jump back on our bikes to head back to the witch's house to pick up the football. Roger shouts. I have about a six-foot head start on him, so I begin pedaling as fast as I can.

"No, Marc! Watch out!" Roger squeals in a panic. I look up just in time to see a black car speeding directly at me through the red light. I leap from my bike. But it's too late.

My lanky fifteen-year-old body smashes into the windshield, flips over the roof of the car, and strikes the concrete with a sickening thud.

I vaguely hear Roger's voice crying for help over the sound of screeching tires as the black car speeds away from the scene of the accident.

Our Guardian Angel

I open my eyes slowly and my vision gradually comes into focus.

"Hey, honey," my mom says.

"Where am I?"

"You're in the hospital, dear. But the surgeon said you're going to be just fine."

"Surgery?"

"You cracked four of your ribs, which punctured your lungs. But they went in and stitched you back together."

"That . . . that . . ."

My mom interrupts me as tears begin rolling down her cheeks. "We just need to be grateful . . . because you were barely breathing, honey. The surgeon said your lungs were filled with blood. He said it could have been a lot worse had the ambulance not gotten to you in time."

"That car . . . that black car . . . it ran the red light," I whisper restlessly.

"Shhh . . . It's OK," my mom reassures me. "The same wonderful man that called the ambulance also called the police with the license plate number of the black car. The driver was drunk. It was a hit-and-run. But the police already have him in custody."

"Do you know who made the calls?"

My mom reaches into her jeans pocket, pulls out a sticky note the paramedics gave her, and holds it up so I can read it: *Chris Evans–305-555-8362.* "Whoever Chris Evans is," my mom says, "he's our guardian angel."

"Have you called him?"

"Yeah, but he doesn't answer my calls. It rings four **times** and goes straight to voicemail. There's not even a voice greeting. I've already left three messages to thank him for saving my baby's life."

How Do You Know?

Six months later, after a grueling recovery process, my doctor finally gives me the nod to partake in regular physical activity again. Roger and I jump at the chance to toss his new Nerf football around at the schoolyard.

"Go deep!" Roger shouts.

"Not yet, dude. I'm still not a hundred percent. My doctor says I need to ease into it slowly. Cool?"

Roger smiles. "Yeah, of course, bro. My bad, I didn't mean to—" He is suddenly interrupted.

"Marc! Marc Andrew something!" a raspy female voice hollers from behind us. Roger and I turn around and are shocked to see the witch lady peeking her head over the schoolyard's fence. "I believe this belongs to you." She holds up my old football and tosses it toward me. The ball bounces across the ground and rolls up to my feet. Sure enough, it's the ball I left on her property the day of the accident.

"Thanks, but . . . how . . . how do you know my name?" I ask.

"Your mom left me a few voicemail messages. My name is Chris Evans," she says.

9 MINDFUL Ways to REMAIN Calm When Others Are Angry

WHEN SOMEONE UPSETS us, it's often because they aren't behaving according to our fantasy of how they "should" behave. The frustration, then, stems not from their behavior but from how their behavior differs from our expectations. This is a moment for looking within.

You can't control how other people behave. You can't control everything that happens to you. What you can control is how you respond to it all. Your power lies in your response. Let's practice, together . . .

1. Get comfortable with pausing.

Don't imagine the worst when you encounter a little drama. When someone is acting irrationally, don't join them by rushing to make a negative judgment call. Instead, pause. Take a deep breath. Give yourself—and the other person—a little extra time and space. Often this is all we need.

2. Respect people's differences.

Choose your battles wisely. And simply agree to disagree sometimes. It is absolutely possible to connect with, and even appreciate the company of, someone you don't completely agree with. When you make a commitment to remain neutral on matters that don't matter that much, or speak respectfully about your disagreements, both parties can remain calm and move forward, in harmony.

3. Be compassionate.

The word "compassion" means "to suffer with." When you can put yourself in the other person's shoes, you give them the space to regroup, without putting any extra pressure on them.

Remember, we never know what's really going on in someone's life. When you interact with others in stressful environments, set an intention to be supportive by leaving the expectations, judgments, and demands at the door.

4. Extend generosity and grace.

Everyone gets upset and loses their temper sometimes. Remind yourself that we are all more alike than we are different. When you catch yourself passing judgment, add "just like me sometimes" to the end of a sentence. For example: *That person is grouchy, just like me sometimes. She is being rude, just like me sometimes.* Choose to let things *go*. Let others off the hook. Take the high road today.

5. Don't take people's behavior personally.

If you take everything personally, you will be offended for the rest of your life. And there's no reason for it. Even when it seems personal, rarely do people do things because of you, they do things because of them. You may not be able to control all the things people say and do to you, but you can decide not to be reduced by them. Make that decision for yourself today. Do what it takes to remain calm and address the situation from the inside out. That's where your greatest power lies.

6. Talk less and learn to appreciate silence.

Don't say things you'll regret five minutes later for the sake of fighting back. Inhale. Exhale. A moment of silence can save you from a hundred moments of regret. Truth be told, you are often most powerful and influential in an argument when you are most silent.

7. Create a morning ritual that starts your day off right.

Don't rush into your day by checking your phone or e-mail. Don't put yourself in a stressful state of mind that will make you incapable of dealing positively with other people's negativity. Create time and space for a morning ritual that's focused and peaceful. Take ten deep breaths, stretch, meditate. When you begin the day mindfully, you lay the foundation for your day being calm and centered, regardless of what's going on around you.

8. Cope using healthy choices and alternatives.

When we face stressful situations, we often calm or soothe ourselves with unhealthy choices—drinking alcohol, eating sugary snacks, smoking, and so on. It's easy to respond to anger with anger and unhealthy distractions.

Notice how you cope with stress. Replace bad coping habits with healthy ones. Take a walk in a green space. Make a cup of tea and sit quietly with your thoughts. Listen to music. Write in your journal. Talk it out with a close friend. Healthy coping habits make happy people.

9. Remind yourself of what's right, and create more of it in the world.

Keeping the positive in mind helps you move beyond the negativity around you.

At the end of the day, reflect on your small daily wins and all the little things that are going well. Count three small events on your fingers that happened during the day that you're undoubtedly grateful for.

And pay it forward when you get a chance to. Let your positivity empower you to think kindly of others, speak kindly to others, and do kind things for others. Kindness always makes a difference. Create the outcomes others might be grateful for at the end of their day. Be a bigger part of what's right in this world.

20 THINGS to STOP Doing to Others

THERE IS ONE key factor that can either damage your relationships or deepen them: your attitude. If you're hoping to grow and maintain positive relationships in your life, read on. Below you will find a twenty-step attitude adjustment guaranteed to help you do just that.

1. Stop holding grudges.
Grudges are a waste of perfect happiness.

2. Stop complaining.
Instead, use your time and energy to do something about it.

3. Stop meaning what you don't say.
People can't read minds. Communicate regularly and effectively.

4. Stop making it all about you.
The world revolves around the sun, not you. Take a moment to acknowledge this truth on a regular basis.

5. Stop lying.

In the long run, the truth always reveals itself. Either you own up to your actions or your actions will ultimately own you.

6. Stop blaming.

When you blame others for what you're going through, you deny responsibility—you give up your power over that part of your life, and you annoy everyone around you in the process.

7. Stop doubting.

Don't let your self-doubt interfere with other people's dreams. Be supportive, or stay out of the way.

8. Stop interrupting.

Correcting someone when they're blatantly wrong is one thing, but always interjecting your opinions out of turn gets old fast.

9. Stop being selfish.

You get what you put into a relationship. Nothing less, nothing more.

10. Stop judging.

Everyone is fighting their own unique war. You have no clue what they are going through, just like they have no clue what you're going through.

11. Stop gossiping.

Gossiping about others is always lose–lose. It hurts them, and then it hurts your reputation.

12. Stop making promises you can't keep.

Don't overpromise. Instead, overdeliver—to others and yourself.

13. Stop being defensive.

Just because someone sees something differently than you doesn't mean either one of you is wrong. Keep an open mind. Otherwise you'll never discover anything new.

14. Stop comparing people to others.

No two people are alike. Everyone has their own strengths. We are only ever competing against ourselves.

15. Stop expecting people to be perfect.

Perfect is the enemy of good. And genuine goodness is hard to find in this world. Don't overlook it.

16. Stop trying to be everything to everyone.

It's impossible. But making one person smile can change their world. So narrow your focus.

17. Stop cheating others just because you can get away with it.

Just because you can get away with something doesn't mean you should do it. Think bigger. Do what you know in your heart is right.

18. Stop making mountains out of molehills.

People make mistakes. There's no reason to stress out yourself and everyone around you because of it. Ask yourself, "Will this matter in one year's time?" If not, let it go.

19. Stop being dramatic.

Stay out of other people's drama and don't needlessly create your own.

20. Stop giving out advice, and just listen.

Less advice is often the best advice. People don't need lots of advice, they need a listening ear and some positive reinforcement. What they want to know is already somewhere inside of them. They just need time to think, be, and breathe, and continue to explore the undirected journeys that will eventually help them find their direction.

20 THINGS to START Doing in Your Relationships

FAMILY ISN'T ALWAYS blood. They're the people in your life who appreciate having you in theirs—the ones who encourage you to improve in healthy and exciting ways, and who not only embrace who you are now, but also who you want to be. These people—your real family—are the ones who truly matter. Here are twenty tips to help you find and foster these special relationships:

1. Free yourself from negative people.

Relationships should help you, not hurt you. Surround yourself with people who reflect the person you want to be. Choose friends whom you are proud to know, people you admire, who love and respect you—people who make your day a little brighter simply by being in it.

2. Let go of those who are already gone.

We rarely lose friends and lovers, we just gradually figure out who our real ones are. So when people walk away from you, let them go. Your destiny is never tied to anyone who leaves you. It doesn't mean they are bad people, it just means that their part in your story is over.

3. Give people you don't know a fair chance.

Everyone has gone through something that has changed them and forced them to grow. If you give them a chance, you'll find everyone has something amazing to offer. So appreciate the possibility of new relationships as you naturally let go of old ones that no longer work. Trust your judgment. Be ready to learn, be ready for a challenge, and be ready to meet someone who might just change your life forever.

4. Show everyone kindness and respect.

Treat everyone with the same level of respect you would give to your grandfather and the same level of patience you would have with your baby brother. People will notice your kindness.

5. Accept people just the way they are.

In most cases it's impossible to change them anyway, and it's rude to try. So save yourself from needless stress. Instead of trying to change others, give them your support, and lead by example.

6. Encourage others and cheer for them.

Having an appreciation for how amazing the people around you are leads to good places—productive, fulfilling, peaceful places. So be happy for those who are making progress. Be thankful for their blessings, openly. What goes around comes around, and sooner or later the people you're cheering for will start cheering for you.

7. Be your perfectly imperfect self.

We are not perfect for everyone, we are only perfect for those select few people who really take the time to get to know us and love us for who we really are. And to those select few, being our perfectly imperfect self is what they love about us.

8. Forgive people and move forward.

Forgiveness is not saying, "What you did to me is OK." It is saying, "I'm not going to let what you did to me ruin my happiness forever." Forgiveness is the remedy. It doesn't mean you're erasing the past, or forgetting what happened. It means you're letting go of the resentment and pain, and instead choosing to learn from the incident and move on with your life.

9. Do little things for others every day.

You can't be everything to everyone, but you can be everything to a select few. Decide who these people are in your life and treat them like royalty.

10. Pay attention to who your real friends are.

Real friends have an honest heart and will go out of their way to help you when you need it most. Real friends are the ones who know you as you are, understand where you have been, accept who you have become, and still encourage you to grow.

11. Always be loyal.

When it comes to relationships, remaining faithful is never an option but a priority. Loyalty is everything.

12. Stay in better touch with people who matter to you.

Stay connected with those who matter to you. Not because it's convenient, but because they're worth the extra effort. Remember, you don't need a certain number of friends, just a number of friends you can be certain of. Paying attention to these people is a priority.

13. Keep your promises and tell the truth.

Lying, cheating, and screwing with people's feelings and emotions hurts. Never mess with someone's feelings just because you're unsure of yours.

14. Give what you want to receive.

Don't expect what you are not willing to give. Start practicing the Golden Rule. If you want love, give love. If you want friends, be friendly. If you want money, provide value.

15. Say what you mean and mean what you say.

Don't try to read other people's minds, and don't make other people try to read yours. Most problems, big and small, within a family, friendship, or business relationship, start with bad communication.

16. Allow others to make their own decisions.

Do not judge others by your own past. What might be good for one person might not be good for another. What might be bad for one person might change another person's life for the better.

17. Talk less and listen more.

Support the people you love—don't stage-manage them. Often what they need is the space to hear their own inner voice.

18. Leave petty arguments behind.

There are many roads to what's right. And most of the time it just doesn't matter.

19. Ignore unconstructive, hurtful commentary.

No matter what you do, there will always be someone who thinks differently. So concentrate on doing what you know in your heart is right. What most people think and say about you isn't all that important. What is important is how you feel about yourself.

20. Pay attention to your relationship with yourself.

One of the most painful things in life is losing yourself in the process of loving others too much, and forgetting that you are special too.

15 THINGS REAL
Friends Do Differently

AS WE MATURE, we realize it becomes less important to have more friends and more important to have real ones. Remember, life is kind of like a party. You invite a lot of people, some leave early, some laugh with you, and a few stay to help you clean up the mess. The ones who stay are your real friends in life. They are the ones who matter most. Here are fifteen things real friends do differently:

1. They face problems together.

A real friend is someone who sees the pain in your eyes while everyone else still believes the smile on your face. Don't look for someone who will solve all your problems; look for someone who will face them with you.

2. They give what they can because they truly care.

One of the biggest challenges in relationships comes from the fact that many of us enter a relationship in order to get something. We try to find someone who's going to make us feel good. In reality, the only way a relationship will last, and give us joy in the long term, is if we see our relationship as a place we go to give, and not just a place we go to take.

Yes, of course it is OK to take something from a relationship too. But both sides should be giving. It can only be a "give and take" if *both sides* are *giving*. That's the key.

3. They make time for each other.

It's obvious, but any relationship without clear communication is going to have problems. In fact, the single greatest problem in communication is the illusion that it has taken place.

4. They offer each other freedom.

A healthy relationship keeps the doors and windows wide open. Plenty of air is circulating and no one feels trapped. Relationships thrive in this environment. Keep your doors and windows open. If this person is meant to be in your life, all the open doors and windows in the world won't make them leave.

5. They communicate effectively.

It's been said many times before, but it's true: great communication is the cornerstone of a great relationship. If you have resentment, you must talk it out rather than let the resentment grow. If you are jealous, you must communicate in an open and honest manner to address your insecurities. If you have expectations of your partner, you must communicate them. If there are any problems whatsoever, you must communicate them and work them out. And communicate more than just problems—communicate the good things too.

6. They accept each other as is.

Trying to change a person never works. People know when they are not accepted in their entirety, and it hurts. A real friend is someone who truly knows you, and loves you just the same. Don't change so people will like you. Be yourself and the right people will love the real you. If you feel like changing something about your friend, ask yourself what change you can make in yourself instead.

7. They are genuine, and expect genuineness.

Don't play games with people's heads and hearts. Remember, love and friendship don't hurt. Lying, cheating, and screwing with people's feelings and emotions hurts. Always be open, honest, and genuine.

8. They compromise.

Real friends meet in the middle. When there's a disagreement, they work out a solution that works for both parties—a compromise, rather than a need for the other person to change or completely give in.

9. They support each other's growth changes.

Our needs change with time. When someone says, "You've changed," it's not always a bad thing. Sometimes it just means you've grown. Don't apologize for it. Instead, be open and sincere, explain how you feel, and keep doing what you know in your heart is right.

10. They believe in each other.

Simply believing in another person, and showing it in your words and deeds, can make a huge difference in their life. Studies of people who grew up in dysfunctional homes but who grew up to be happy and successful show that the one thing they had in common was someone who believed in them. Do this for those you care about. Support their dreams and passions and hobbies. Participate with them. Cheer for them. Be nothing but encouraging. Whether they actually accomplish these dreams or not, your belief is of infinite importance to them.

11. They maintain realistic expectations of their relationship.

Notice when you're projecting something onto the other person that has nothing to do with them, and make an effort to let it go. Recognize when you're looking for that person to do something for you that you need to do for yourself, and release those expectations and look inside instead.

12. They honor each other in small ways on a regular basis.

Every day you have the opportunity to make your relationship sweeter and deeper by making small gestures to show your appreciation and affection. Make an effort to really listen—not just wait to talk. See the other person as if for the first time. It's all too easy to take someone for granted. Really notice all the wonderful things they do, and let them know what you see.

13. They listen, and they hear every word.

Giving a person a voice, and showing them that their words matter, will have a long-lasting impact on them—and the trust you're building between you.

14. They keep their promises.

Your word means everything. Real friends keep promises and tell the truth up front.

15. They stick around.

The sad truth is that there are some people who will only be there for you as long as you have something they need. When you no longer serve a purpose for them, they will leave. The good news is, if you tough it out, you'll eventually weed these people out of your life and be left with some great people you can count on.

12 Relationship TRUTHS We Often Forget

IT'S EASY TO make your relationships more complicated than they are. Here are twelve simple reminders to help you keep them on course:

1. All successful relationships require some work.

They don't just happen, or maintain themselves. They exist and thrive when the parties involved take the risk of sharing what it is that's going on in their minds and hearts.

2. Most of the time you get what you put in.

If you want love, give love. If you'd like to feel understood, try being more understanding. It's a simple practice that works.

3. You shouldn't have to fight for a spot in someone's life.

Never force someone to make a space in their life for you, because if they know your worth, they will create one for you.

4. There is a purpose for everyone you meet.

Some people will test you, some will use you, and some will teach you, but most important, some will bring out the best in you. Learn to see and accept the differences between these people, and carry on accordingly.

5. We all change, and that's OK.

Our needs change with time. Healthy relationships always move in the direction of growth—for the relationship as a whole and for each individual in it. When you connect with a true friend or partner, this person helps you find the best in yourself. In this way, you both grow into your best selves.

6. You are in control of your own happiness.

If your relationship with yourself isn't working, don't expect your other relationships to be any different. Nobody else in this world can make you happy. It's something you have to do on your own. And you have to create your own happiness first before you can share it with someone else. If you feel that it's your partner's fault, think again and look within yourself to find out what piece is missing. The longing for completion that you feel inside comes from being out of touch with who you are.

7. Forgiving others helps you.

Forgive others, not because they deserve forgiveness, but because you deserve peace. Free yourself of the burden of being an eternal victim. When you choose to forgive those who have hurt you, you take away their power over you.

8. You can't change people; they can only change themselves.

Instead of trying to change others, give them your support and lead by example. If there's a specific behavior someone you love has that you're hoping disappears over time, accept that it probably won't. If you really need them to change something, be honest and put all the cards on the table so this person knows what you need them to do.

9. Heated arguments are a waste of time.

The less time you spend arguing with the people who hurt you, the more time you'll have to love the people who love you. And if you happen to find yourself arguing with someone you love, don't let your anger get the best of you. Give yourself some time to calm down and then gently discuss the situation.

10. You are better off without some people.

When you have to start compromising yourself and your morals for the people around you, it's probably time to change the people around you. If someone continuously mistreats you or pushes you in the wrong direction, have enough respect for yourself to walk away. You'll be OK, and far better off in the long run.

11. Small gestures of kindness go a long way.

Honor your important relationships in some way every chance you get. Every day you have the opportunity to make your relationship sweeter and deeper by making small gestures to show your appreciation and affection. Use your voice for kindness, your ears for compassion, your hands for charity, your mind for truth, and your heart for love. You have the power to improve someone else's day, perhaps even their whole life, simply by giving them your compassion and kindness. Do it!

12. Even the best relationships don't last forever.

Because nothing lasts forever. So look around and be thankful right now, for your family, friends, and the health you all have that allows you to share new life experiences.

15 Relationship TRUTHS for Tough Times

THESE RELATIONSHIP TRUTHS may be a bit difficult to accept at times, but in the end, they will help you weed out the wrong relationships, make room for the right ones, and nurture the people who are most important to you.

1. Some relationships will be blessings, others will serve as lessons.

Either way, never regret knowing someone. Everyone you encounter teaches you something. Some people will test you, some will use you, and some will teach you, but most important, some will bring out the best in you.

2. When times get tough, some people will leave you.

When you are up in life, your friends get to know who you are. When you are down in life, you get to know who your true friends are. There will be lots of people around when times are easy, but take note of who remains in your life when times get tough, especially the people who sacrifice the resources they have in their life to help you improve yours when you need it most. These people are your real friends.

3. Life is full of fake people.

Not everyone has your best interests at heart. But sometimes you have to be tricked and misled by the wrong lovers and friends once or twice in your life in order to find and appreciate your soul mate and real friends when they arrive.

4. People can easily be insincere with their words.

When someone truly loves you, they don't have to say a word. You will be able to tell simply by the way they treat you over the long term. Remember, actions speak much louder than words. A person can say sorry a thousand times, and say "I love you" as much as they want. But if they're not going to prove that the things they say are true, then they're not worth listening to. Because if they can't show it, their words are not sincere.

5. The less you associate with some people, the more your life will improve.

Don't settle for just being someone's downtime, spare time, part time, or sometime. If they can't be there for you all of the time, especially when you need them most, then they're not worth your time.

6. Harsh words can hurt a person more than physical pain.

Taste your own words before you let them out. Words hurt and scar more than you think, so *think* before you speak. And remember, what you say about others also says a whole lot about *you*.

7. A mistake is an accident. Cheating and lying are not mistakes.

They are intentional choices. Stop hiding behind the words "mistake" and "sorry" and stop putting up with those who do.

8. Excessive jealousy doesn't tell someone how much you love them.

It tells them how much you dislike yourself. And no amount of love, or promises, or proof from them will ever be enough to make you feel better. For those broken pieces you carry are pieces you must mend for yourself. Happiness is an inside job.

9. When people get nasty with you, it's usually best to walk away.

When someone treats you like dirt, don't pay attention and don't take it personally. They're saying nothing about you and a lot about themselves. And no matter what they do or say, never drop down to their level and sling dirt back. Just know you're better than that and walk away.

10. People will treat you the way you let them treat you.

You can't control them, but you can control what you tolerate. Beautiful things happen when you distance yourself from negative people. Doing so does not mean you hate them, it simply means you respect yourself.

11. One of the most difficult tasks in life is removing someone from your heart.

But remember, no relationship is a waste of time. The wrong ones teach you the lessons that prepare you for the right ones.

12. Resentment hurts you, not them.

Whisper a small prayer of gratitude for the people who have stuck by your side, and send a prayer of goodwill for those who didn't. For should these people hear your prayers, those who have been there will know how much you appreciate them, and those who left will know that you appreciate your own happiness enough to not let resentment destroy your capacity to live with a compassionate heart.

13. Silence and a half smile can hide a lot of pain from the world.

Everyone you meet is afraid of something, loves something, and has lost something. Know this. You never know what someone has been through, or what they're going through today. Don't make empty judgments about them. Be kind. Ask about their stories. Listen.

14. True love comes when manipulation stops.

True love comes when you care more about who the other person really is than about who you think they should become, when you dare to reveal yourself honestly, and when you dare to be open and vulnerable. It takes two to create a sincere environment where this is possible. If you haven't found true love yet, don't settle. There is someone out there who will share true love with you, even if it's not the person you were initially hoping for.

15. Even the best relationships don't last forever.

Nobody gets through life without losing someone they love. Appreciate what you have, who loves you and who cares for you. You'll never know how much they mean to you until the day they are no longer beside you. And remember, just because something doesn't last forever doesn't mean it wasn't worth your while.

10 SIGNS It's TIME to Let Go

HOLDING ON CAN be brave, but letting go and moving on is often what makes us stronger and happier. Here are ten signs it's time to let go:

1. Someone expects you to be someone you're not.

Don't change who you are for anyone else. It's wiser to lose someone over being who you are than to keep them by being someone you're not. It's easier to fill an empty space in your life where someone else used to be than it is to fill the empty space inside yourself where *you* used to be.

2. A person's actions don't match their words.

Everyone deserves someone who helps them look forward to tomorrow. If someone has the opposite effect on you because they are consistently inconsistent and their actions don't match up with their words, it's time to let them go. It's always better to be alone than to be in bad company. Don't listen to what people say; watch what they do. Your true friends will slowly reveal themselves over time.

3. You catch yourself trying to force someone to love you.

Let us keep in mind that we can't force anyone to love us. We shouldn't beg someone to stay when they want to leave. That's what love is all about—freedom. However, the end of love is not the end of life. It should be the beginning of an understanding that love sometimes leaves for a reason, but never leaves without a lesson. Sometimes it takes a while to find the right person, but the right person is always worth the wait.

4. An intimate relationship is based strictly on physical attraction.

Being beautiful is more than how others perceive you at a single glance. It's about what you live for. It's about what defines you. It's about the depth of your heart, and what makes you unique. People who are only attracted to you because of your pretty face or nice body won't stay by your side forever. But the people who can see how beautiful your heart is will never leave you.

5. Someone continuously breaks your trust.

Love means giving someone the chance to hurt you but trusting them not to. In the end you'll discover who's fake, who's true, and who would risk it all for you.

6. Someone continuously overlooks your worth.

There comes a point when you have to let go and stop chasing some people. If someone wants you in their life, they'll find a way to put you there. Sometimes you just need to let go and accept the fact that they don't care for you the way you care for them. We think it's too hard to let go, until we actually do. Then we ask ourselves, "Why didn't I do this sooner?"

7. You are never given a chance to speak your mind.

Sometimes an argument saves a relationship, whereas silence breaks it. Speak up for your heart so that you won't have regrets. Life is not about making others happy. Life is about being honest and sharing your happiness with others.

8. You are frequently forced to sacrifice your happiness.

If you allow people to make more withdrawals than deposits in your life, you will be out of balance and in the negative before you know it. Know when to close the account. It's always better to be alone with dignity than in a relationship that constantly requires you to sacrifice your happiness and self-respect.

9. You truly dislike your current situation.

Too many people spend their lives climbing the ladder of success only to reach the top and discover that the ladder was leaning against the wrong wall. Don't be one of them. It's always better to be at the bottom of the ladder you actually want to climb than the top of the one you don't.

10. You catch yourself obsessing over, and living in, the past.

Eventually you will overcome the heartache, and forget the reasons you cried, and who caused the pain. Eventually you will realize that the secret to happiness and freedom is not about control or revenge, but in letting things unfold naturally, and learning from your experiences over the course of time. So let go of the past, set yourself free, and open your mind to the possibility of new relationships and priceless experiences.

20 Morning Mantras to START the Day LOVING PEOPLE (Instead of JUDGING or IGNORING Them)

SINCE WE ALL intellectually understand that we shouldn't bypass or judge people too quickly, but sometimes still forget when we're in the heat of a pressing moment, we recommend reading (and rereading) the following morning mantras to yourself at least a couple times a week:

1. The most beautiful thing is to see a person nearby smiling. And even more beautiful is knowing that you are the reason behind it.

2. If you have the power to make someone happier today, do it. The world needs more of that.

3. Some people build lots of walls in their lives and not enough bridges. There's no good reason to be one of them. Open yourself up. Take small chances on people.

4. Never stop doing little things for those around you. Sometimes those little things occupy the biggest part of their hearts.

5. Too often we underestimate the power of a touch, a smile, a kind word, a listening ear, an honest compliment, or the smallest act of love— all of which have the potential to turn a life around.

6. Be present. Be thoughtful. Compliment people. Magnify their strengths, not their weaknesses. This is how to make a real and lasting difference in your relationships, new and old.

7. We don't always need advice. Sometimes all we need is a hand to hold, an ear to listen, and a heart to understand.

8. Today, just be 100 percent present with those around you—*be all there*. That is enough.

9. There's no such thing as "self-made." Someone else believed in you. Someone else encouraged you. Someone else invested in you. Someone else prayed for you. Someone else spoke life over you. Be that someone for others too.

10. It's practically impossible to love our neighbors if we don't know them, and yet that's oftentimes the case. We live in such a hyper-connected world with such limited or nonexistent connection. Remember this: Relationships matter. Stories matter.

11. In human relationships, distance is not measured in miles but in affection. Two people can be right next to each other yet miles apart.

12. Stay in touch with those who truly matter to you—not because it's convenient, but because they're worth the extra effort.

13. The single greatest problem in communication is the illusion that it has taken place. Too often we don't listen to understand, we listen to reply. Bring awareness to this. And listen for what's truly behind the words.

14. Set an example. Treat everyone with respect, even those who are rude to you—not because they are always nice, but because *you* are. (And do your best to be thankful for the rude and difficult people too; they serve as great reminders of how not to be.)

15. Sometimes it is better to be kind than to be right.

16. People are much nicer when they're happier, which says a lot about those who aren't very nice to you. Sad, but true.

17. The real test always comes when you don't get what you expect from people. Will you react in anger? Or will calmness be your superpower?

18. The way we treat people we don't understand is a report card on what we've learned about love, compassion, and kindness.

19. Be kinder than necessary. What goes around comes around. No one has ever made themselves strong by showing how small someone else is.

20. The best relationships are not just about the good times you share, they're also about the obstacles you go through together, and the fact that you still say "I love you" in the end.

Afterthoughts on "Loving" Offensive People

Some of the morning mantras above (such as numbers 14 through 19, for example) potentially require a willingness to cordially deal with people who yell at us, interrupt us, cut us off in traffic, talk about distasteful things, and so forth.

These people violate the way we think people should behave. And sometimes their behavior deeply offends us.

But if we let these people get to us again and again, we will be upset and offended far too often.

So, what can we do?

There isn't a one-size-fits-all solution, but here are two strategies we often recommend to our course students:

- **Be bigger, think bigger.** Imagine a two-year-old who doesn't get what she wants at the moment. She throws a temper tantrum! This small, momentary problem is enormous in her little mind because she lacks perspective on the situation. But as adults, we know better. We realize that there are dozens of other things this two-year-old could do to be happier. Sure, that's easy for us to say—we have a bigger perspective, right? But when someone offends us, our bigger perspective suddenly shrinks again—this small, momentary offense seems enormous, and it makes us want to scream. We throw the equivalent of a two-year-old's temper tantrum. However, if we think bigger, we can see that this small thing matters very little in the grand scheme of things. It's not worth our energy. So always remind yourself to be bigger, think bigger, and broaden your perspective.

- **Mentally hug them and wish them better days.** This little trick can positively change the way we see people who offend us. Let's say someone has just said something unpleasant to us. How dare they! Who do they think they are? They have no consideration for our feelings! But of course, with a heated reaction like this, we're not having any consideration for their feelings either—they may be suffering inside in unimaginable ways. By remembering this, we can try to show them empathy and realize that their behavior is likely driven by some kind of inner pain. They are being unpleasant as a coping mechanism for their pain. And so, mentally, we can give them a hug. We can have compassion for this broken person, because we all have been broken and in pain at some point too. We're the same in many ways. Sometimes we need a hug, some extra compassion, and a little unexpected love.

Try one of these strategies the next time someone offends you. And then smile in serenity, armed with the comforting knowledge that there's no reason to let someone else's behavior turn you into someone you aren't.

RELATIONSHIP QUESTIONS
TO MAKE YOU THINK

Have you been the KIND of friend you want as a *friend*?

Which is WORSE, when a *good* friend moves away, or losing touch with a *good* friend who lives right near you?

What can you do TODAY to become a *person* others want to be around?

What are the top three QUALITIES you look for in a *friend*?

What are you known for by your FRIENDS and *family*?

Have you ever been with someone, said nothing, and walked away feeling like you just had the BEST *conversation* ever?

Whom do you LOVE? What are you *doing* about it?

Is it POSSIBLE to *lie* without saying a word?

Would you break the law to SAVE a *loved* one?

If you knew that everyone you know was going to die tomorrow, WHOM would you *visit* today?

. . . . .

PART FOUR

Self-Love

Never forget,
YOU deserve YOUR love and affection just as much,
if not more, than anyone else in the universe.

WE ARE ALL WEIRD

DURING MY COMPETITIVE cross-country running days it wasn't uncommon for me to run five miles at five a.m. and another ten miles at ten p.m., six days a week. I was competitive. I wanted to win races. And I was smart enough to know that if I dedicated myself to extra training, while my opponents were sleeping or socializing, I would be one step ahead of them when we crossed the finish line.

Over time, I became quite proficient at doing this. I got so good at it, in fact, that I actually looked forward to running. Because when I ran, my mind was clear and at peace with the world—especially when nobody else was around. In the midst of what seemed to be a strenuous workout, my mind was in a soothingly relaxed state . . . similar to that of a deep meditation.

I don't compete in races anymore, but I still run almost every day. Even though I no longer have to, I typically still run in the wee hours of the morning or very late at night. And since my friends know that I have a flexible work schedule, most of them think I'm a bit weird for running at such "odd" hours. I've tried to explain to them why I do it, and how it soothes my mind. But they can't relate. So I'm still a weirdo in their eyes.

A Memorable Encounter

Recently I went running on the Pacific Beach Boardwalk at eleven p.m. It was calm and quiet out—just the way I like it. I was about three miles into my run when a peculiar-looking woman sitting on the boardwalk's barrier wall shouted, "Hey, you!" and then waved me down. My first inclination was to just ignore her and continue running. But my curiosity got the best of me. So I stopped.

The woman had long blonde dreadlocks, several piercings in her ears and nose, tattoos on both arms, and a Grateful Dead T-shirt on. She was strumming an acoustic guitar and had a thick, white joint burning in a small ashtray beside her.

She stopped strumming her guitar and began to chuckle as soon as she saw me looking down at the joint. "Don't worry," she said, "I'm legit. I have a medical prescription for it."

"It's none of my business," I quickly replied.

"Anyway," she continued, "perhaps you don't realize this, but it's pretty late to be out exercising. I've seen you out here a few times before, running after midnight."

"So, what's your point?" I asked.

"Well, thousands of people run on this boardwalk every single day, but you seem to be the only runner I see in the middle of the night. And it strikes me as being kind of weird. So, what's your deal?"

I told her about my love for a quiet landscape, and the way that running soothes my mind—". . . like a deep mediation," I told her.

She smiled, strummed once on her guitar, and took a drag of her joint. "Well, then, I'm doing the same thing as you right now," she replied. "Only in my own way—a way that works for me. Can you dig that?"

I stared at her for a second and then laughed, because I knew she was right. "Yeah, I can dig that," I said. She winked and started strumming her guitar again. I winked back and started running again.

Looking Deeper

Some of us run in the middle of the night. Some of us strum acoustic guitars and smoke joints. And others go to church. Or sip expensive wine. Or surf on dangerous waves. Or jump out of perfectly good airplanes. When we try to understand people by personally relating to the things that they do, we usually can't make any sense of it. Because it's easier to see weirdness in a sea of normality than it is to decode the logical methods behind one's madness.

But when we look just a little deeper, by making a noble effort to understand people by truly listening to why they do the things that they do, they never seem quite as weird. Actually, they begin to seem . . .

Almost normal.

10 TRUTHS That Will Change the Way You SEE YOURSELF Today

I SAT AT the kitchen table staring at her through tear-filled eyes. "I feel crazy," I said. "I don't know what's wrong with me!"

"Why do you feel crazy?" she asked.

"Because I'm neurotic and self-conscious and ashamed, and so much more all at once," I said. "I feel like I'm just not good enough for anything or anyone anymore . . ."

"And you don't think everyone feels like this at times?" she asked.

"Not like this," I replied under my breath.

"Well, you're wrong," she said. "If you think you know someone who never feels a bit broken and crazy, you just don't know enough about them. Every one of us contains a measure of 'crazy' that moves us in strange, often perplexing ways. This side of us is necessary; it's part of our human ability to think, grieve, adapt, and grow. It's part of being alive and intelligent."

I sat silently for a moment. My eyes gazed from her eyes to the ground and back to her eyes again. "So, you're saying I should *want* to feel like this?"

"To an extent," she said. "Let me put it this way: Taking all your feelings seriously all the time, and letting them drive you into misery, is a waste of your amazing spirit. You have to know that sometimes what you feel simply won't align with what's true and right in this world; it's just your subconscious mind's way of allowing you to look at things from a different perspective. These feelings will come and go as long as you let them go . . . as long as you consciously see them for what they are."

We shared another moment of silence, then my lips curled up slightly and I cracked a smile. "Thank you, Grandma," I said.

Why We Belittle Ourselves

That conversation with my grandmother took place on a warm September evening more than two decades ago. I remember it vividly because I was smart enough to write a five-page journal entry about it immediately afterward. And what I wrote continues to remind me of how easy it is to fall into a self-deprecating state of mind—to subconsciously belittle oneself when times get tough. For instance, over the years I can't even begin to tell you how many times I've caught myself thinking, "You're not good enough!" simply because I wasn't having a good day.

Can you relate at all?

To an extent, I bet you can. Because we all do this to ourselves sometimes . . .

You have a story about yourself (or perhaps a series of them) that you recite to yourself daily. This is your mental movie, and it's a feature film that plays on repeat in your mind. Your movie is about who you are: you have a chubby tummy, your skin is too dark, you aren't smart, you aren't lovable . . . you aren't good enough. Start to pay attention when your movie plays—when you feel anxiety about being who you are—because it affects everything you do. Realize that this movie isn't real, it isn't true, and it isn't you. It's just a train of thought that can be stopped—a script that can be rewritten.

Ready to rewrite the script? Good!

Choose to remind yourself of the truth . . .

1. You are not what happened to you. You are not your past experiences. You are not your scars. You are not what someone else once said about you. You are what you choose to become in this moment. Let go, breathe, and begin again today.

2. You are more than that one broken piece of you. We all have this image in our minds of ourselves—this idea of who we are. And when this idea gets chipped or broken in some small way, we tend to broadly internalize it. It's easy to feel like everything—*all* of you—is broken along with that one small piece of you. But that's not true. Because you are more than one thing—you are many things! And remembering this can help you stretch your identity so it's not so fragile—so it doesn't shatter when a small piece of it gets chipped.

3. Other people's opinions of you are rarely accurate. People may have heard your stories, but they can't feel what you are going through today. They aren't living your life! So, let go of what they say about you. There is great freedom in leaving others to their opinions. And there is a huge weight lifted when you take nothing personally.

4. You are as worthy as you believe yourself to be. You will never find your worth in another human being—you find it in yourself, and then you will attract those who are worthy of your energy. Accept and acknowledge your own worth today. Stop waiting for others to tell you how important you are. Tell yourself right now. And believe it.

5. The best time to be extra kind to yourself is when you don't feel like it. That's when doing so can make the biggest difference. Truly, it's not what you say to everybody else that determines your life, it's what you whisper to yourself every day that has the greatest power.

6. It's not too late. You aren't behind—you are exactly where you need to be. Every step is necessary. Don't judge or berate yourself for how long your journey is taking. We all need our own time to travel our own distance.

7. You have come a long way. The trick is to embrace life today. Don't wish it away waiting for better days ahead. Just appreciate where you are. You've come a long way, and you're still learning and growing. Be thankful for the lessons. Give yourself credit for your resilience, and step forward again with grace.

8. It's OK to not feel OK sometimes. Sometimes not being OK is all we can register inside our weary minds and aching hearts. This feeling is human, and accepting it can feel like a small weight lifted. Truth be told, it's not OK when someone you care about is no longer breathing and giving their amazing gifts to the world. It's not OK when someone you trusted betrays you and breaks your heart. It's not OK when you're emotionally drained. It's not OK when you're engulfed in grief like you've never known before. Whatever the latest painful season of life consists of, sometimes it's just *not* OK right now. And that realization is more than OK. Breathe . . .

9. You need to distance yourself to see your situation clearly. Step back. Give yourself space. Sometimes the most important thing you do in a whole day is the short rest you take between two deep breaths. Take those breaths, and that rest, when you need them. Just let go for a moment and remind yourself that the strongest sign of your growth is knowing you're slightly less stressed by the hard realities that used to absolutely overwhelm you.

10. You are a work in progress. When you feel like you're running in circles, remember that we all feel like this sometimes, especially when life's demands are high and the work is challenging. This doesn't mean you should give up. Make adjustments as necessary, but keep putting one foot in front of the other. You are not really running in circles; you are running upward, gradually. The path is just a spiral set of steps, and you have already climbed higher than you realize. So be a work in progress today, and celebrate how far you've come.

Your Real Story Has Strengthened You

Let the truth sink in. And then remind yourself of it—read the reminders above—again and again, anytime you catch yourself belittling yourself. Bring awareness to the false, self-deprecating story—that mental movie—you're so used to reciting. Then rewrite the script . . . One day at a time. One reminder at a time. Change the way you see yourself.

12 LIES to Stop Telling Yourself

THE WORST LIES are the ones we subconsciously tell ourselves. They've been ingrained in our minds by bad external influences and negative thinking. So the next time you decide to unclutter your life and clean up your space, start with your emotional space by clearing out the old lies and negative self-talk you often recite to yourself. Here are twelve lies to stop telling yourself:

1. I don't have enough yet to be happy.
The happiest of people aren't the luckiest, and they usually don't have the best of everything; they just make the most of everything that comes their way. The reason so many people give up is because they tend to look at what's missing and how far they still have to go, instead of what's present and how far they have come.

2. My dreams are impossible.
Don't let someone who gave up on their dreams talk you out of going after yours. The best thing you can do in life is follow your heart. Take risks. Let your dreams be bigger than your fears and your actions speak

louder than your words. Do something every day that your future self will thank you for.

3. I am stuck with people who hurt me.

If someone continuously mistreats you, have enough respect for yourself to leave them. It may hurt for a while, but it'll be OK. You'll be OK. Oftentimes, walking away has nothing to do with weakness, and everything to do with strength.

4. My failed relationships were a waste of time.

There are certain people who aren't meant to fit into your life. But no relationship is ever a waste of time. If it doesn't bring you what you want, it teaches you what you *don't* want. It just takes a little time to figure it all out.

5. Things will never get better.

Living means facing problems, learning, adapting, and solving them over the course of time. This is what ultimately molds us into the person we become. When you find yourself cocooned in isolation and cannot find your way out of the darkness, remember that this is similar to the place where caterpillars go to grow their wings.

6. Failure is bad.

Sometimes you have to fail a thousand times to succeed. No matter how many mistakes you make or how slowly you progress, you are still way ahead of everyone who isn't trying. Don't get so hung up on one failed attempt that you miss the opening for many more. And remember, failure is not falling down, failure is staying down when you have the choice to get back up.

7. Great things will come to me effortlessly.

Never leave your key to happiness in someone else's pocket, and don't wait on someone else to build your dream life for you. Be the architect and keeper of your own happiness. The more you take responsibility for your past and present, the more you are able to create the future you seek.

8. My past is 100 percent indicative of my future.

At some point, we've all made mistakes, been walked out on, used, and forgotten. But we shouldn't regret one moment of it, because in those moments we've learned a lot from our bad choices. And even though there are some things we can never recover and people who will never be sorry, we now know better for next time.

9. I never need to meet anyone new.

It sounds harsh, but you cannot keep every friend you've ever made. People and priorities change. As some relationships fade, others will grow. Appreciate the possibility of new relationships as you naturally let go of old ones that no longer work. Embrace new relationships. Be ready to learn, be ready for a challenge, and be ready to meet someone who might just change your life forever.

10. I can't live without those who are gone.

Life is change. People really do come and go. Some come back, some don't, and that's OK. And just because one person leaves doesn't mean you should forget about everyone else who's still standing by your side. Continue to appreciate what you have, and smile as you embrace the memories.

11. I'm not ready because I'm not good enough yet.

Nobody ever feels 100 percent ready when an opportunity arises. Most great opportunities in life force us to grow beyond our comfort zone, which means we won't feel totally comfortable at first. Stop berating yourself for being a work in progress. Start embracing it! You are ready. You just need to start.

12. I have way too much to lose.

In the end you will not regret the things you have done nearly as much as the things you have left undone. It's better to think "Oh, well" than "What if."

10 THINGS to TELL Yourself Today

LAUGH WHEN YOU can. Cry when you need to. Focus on your priorities. Make decisions, not excuses. And always stay true to your values. Yes, today is the perfect day to stand up and say:

1. I am fighting hard for the things I want most.
The harder you have to fight for something, the more it will be worth to you once you achieve it. Most great things don't come easy, but they are worth waiting for and fighting for.

2. I am taking action now.
Many great things can be done in a day if you don't always make that day tomorrow. Don't let your fear of making a mistake stop you from getting started.

3. I am focusing on the next positive step.
We sometimes face situations that can stop us dead in our tracks, frozen with fear. We can either stay stuck in that place, or we can gently remove our attention from whatever is happening and focus instead on our next step—on what is possible now.

4. I am proud to wear my truth.

How you see yourself means everything. To be beautiful means to live confidently in your own skin. Say it, and then say it again: "This is my life, my choices, my mistakes, and my lessons. Not yours."

5. I have a lot to smile about.

Happiness is not a result of getting something you don't have, but rather of recognizing and appreciating what you do have. You create happiness with your attitude, your behavior, and your actions. It is all up to you.

6. I am making the best of it.

Everything you go through grows you. Let each day be a scavenger hunt in which you must find at least one of these things: a sincere laugh, an act of kindness, a realization, or a lesson that will lead you closer to your dreams.

7. I am letting go of yesterday's stress.

Sometimes the reason it's so hard for us to be happy is simply because we refuse to let go of the things that make us upset. As the sun sets on this day, let it go. Leave behind the stress, the drama, and the worries. Tomorrow is about hope, new possibilities, and the opportunity to make a better day.

8. There is enough time today to do something I love.

Where did you leave your happiness? With an old lover? In a city where you once lived? In a story you never finished writing? In a dream you gave up on? In a hope you got too weary to carry? Wherever you left it, go back and retrieve it. If you don't remember where you left it, dedicate a little time today to doing something you love to do, and you will find your happiness somewhere nearby.

9. I am priceless in someone's eyes.

Being with someone who overlooks your worth isn't loyalty, it's a total waste of what could be. Focus on those who love and accept you for who you are, and shower them with the love and kindness they deserve. And above all, cherish the people who saw you when you were invisible to everyone else.

10. It's not too late.

No matter who you are, no matter what you did, no matter where you've come from, you can always change and become a better version of yourself. Peace, strength, and direction will come to you when you manage to tune out the noisy judgments of others in an effort to better hear the soft and steady hum of your own inner strength. And once you hear it, you will realize that it's not too late to be what you might have been.

17 DEADLIEST Decisions You Can Make

WHEN THE DEEPEST part of you becomes engaged in what you are doing, when what you do serves both yourself and others, you are living life the way it is meant to be lived. But it's easy to get off track. Sometimes it's the smallest decisions that can change your life forever. Here are some seemingly small but damaging decisions to avoid on your journey forward:

1. Not loving what is

Love what you do, until you can do what you love. Love where you are, until you can be where you love. Love the people you are with, until you can be with the people you love most. This is the way we find happiness.

2. Waiting and waiting and waiting

Good things don't come to those who wait. Good things come to those who pursue the goals and dreams they believe in. "Coulda, woulda, shoulda . . ." Stop it! Don't blame your past for what you don't have. Instead, look at your present. Ask yourself, "What can I do *now* that will bring me closer to where I want to be?"

3. Changing who you are because others have changed

People change. Accept it. Wish them well. Be happy anyway. If you're being true to yourself and it isn't enough for the people around you, change the people around you.

4. Letting heartache define you

Don't allow your temporary wounds to permanently transform you into someone you aren't. A strong person is not the one who doesn't cry. A strong person is the one who cries openly for a moment, and then gets up and fights again for what they believe in.

5. Running away from problems

It doesn't matter who you used to be; what matters is who you are today. What you do *today* can improve all of your tomorrows. So don't run; instead, do something that creates positive change.

6. Being ungrateful

Even in the most peaceful surroundings, the ungrateful heart finds trouble. Even in the most troublesome surroundings, the grateful heart finds peace. Choose to see the world through grateful eyes; it will never look the same again.

7. Allowing long-term anger to occupy your heart

The best medicine is a strong dose of love, laughter, and letting go. Don't allow even a tiny bit of anger to live in your heart.

8. Believing that beauty looks a certain way

We're taught to believe that miniature waists and perfect tans are beautiful. But the truth is that originality is beautiful: Your voice, your laugh, and your personality. Every inch of you that shines with your unique essence. You're truly beautiful, just like the rest of us.

9. Letting your expectations run rampant

Everyone has their own challenges, everyone has their own journey. It is meaningless to compare one with the other. Always love and accept the real people in front of you, not the fantasy of who you hope and wish these people could become.

10. Disrespecting others

No matter what happens in life, be good to the people around you. If you do, you'll leave a great legacy behind regardless of the dreams and ideals you choose to pursue.

11. Disrespecting yourself

Being kind to yourself in thoughts, words, and actions is just as important as being kind to others. The most painful thing is losing yourself in the process of loving others, and forgetting that you are special too.

12. Letting your expectations of others overwhelm you

Don't lower your standards, but do remember that removing your expectations of others is the best way to avoid being disappointed by them. The truth is, others won't always do for us what we do for them.

13. Rushing love

Don't settle. Find someone who isn't afraid to admit they miss you. Someone who knows you're not perfect, but treats you as you are. One who gives their heart completely. Someone who says, "I love you," and then shows it. Find someone who wouldn't mind waking up with you in the morning, seeing your wrinkles and gray hair, and falling in love with you all over again.

14. Neglecting your most important relationships

Relationships built on a foundation of love and respect can weather many storms. This foundation can be checked, maintained, and kept healthy with generous doses of acceptance, forgiveness, listening, gratitude, and considerate actions.

15. Trying to control every last detail about everything

Sometimes it's better not to assume, not to wonder, not to imagine, and not to obsess. Just breathe, do what you can, and have faith that everything will work out for the best.

16. Never taking risks

Life is inherently risky. There is only one risk you should avoid at all costs, and that is the risk of doing nothing. Get out there and make something happen, even if it's just a small step in the right direction.

17. Giving up on you

No matter how many times you break down, there is a little voice inside you that says, "You're not done yet! Get back up!" That's the voice of passion and courage. You are well equipped for the journey of life as long as you tap into your talents and gifts, and allow them to flourish.

12 CHOICES Your FUTURE Self Will Thank You For

WHEN LIFE PUSHES you over, stand up and push back even harder. Where there is a fork in the road and choices to make, make the ones your future self will thank you for. Today, start:

1. Choosing you

The most exhausting activity is pretending to be who you know you aren't. No matter how loud their opinions are, others do not choose who *you* are. Choose *you* even if nobody else is.

2. Appreciating what you have

Sometimes, when you make the most out of what you have, it turns out to be a lot more than you ever imagined. When you wake up, take a moment to think about what a privilege it is to simply be alive and healthy. The moment you start acting like life is a blessing, it will start to feel like one.

3. Believing in yourself and your dreams

Believe in *you*. Listen to your soul. Trust your instincts. Acknowledge your own strengths. Dream it and dare it. Do what you are afraid of, and capable of. Follow your vision. Know that anything is possible. Know you *can*.

4. Being positive

You can't live a positive life with a negative attitude. Let every day be a dream you can touch. Let every day be a love you can feel. Let every day be a reason to live. Life is too short to be anything but positive.

5. Taking action

The happiest and most successful people are usually those who have broken the chains of procrastination, who find satisfaction in doing the job at hand. They're full of eagerness, passion, and productivity. You can be too. Success in life is about *action, action, action*.

6. Letting go

The biggest step in changing the world around you is to change the world within you. Just live in the present, concentrate on the things you can control, and take one small step at a time.

7. Picking yourself back up

Sometimes when things go wrong it's because they would have turned out worse if they had gone right. The only step that matters is the next one you take.

8. Ignoring negative people

You are not a rug; some people may try to walk all over you, but you don't have to lie there and take it. There are seven billion people in the world; don't waste your time by letting one of them ruin your happiness. Simply move on—you're worth it.

9. Staying in touch with close friends and family

There comes a time in life when you'll have to leave everything behind for a while and start something new, but never forget the people who stood by your side, especially your close friends and family who never gave up on you.

10. Making time for fun

Fun is way underrated. With all of life's responsibilities, fun will sometimes seem like an indulgence. But it should be a requirement. Let loose and play. You'll feel happier—now and in the long run.

11. Spreading love and kindness

The happiness surrounding you is greatly affected by the choices you make every day. So choose to spread love and kindness to at least one person a day. Imagine the amount of happiness you can create in a lifetime, day by day.

12. Being the change you want to see in the world

Don't tell others how to live; *live* and let them watch you. Walk the talk. The people who look up to you will likely emulate your actions, so *be* who you want them to be.

10 WAYS to WRITE
a Life Story Worth Living

WHEN WRITING THE story of your life, don't let someone else hold the pen. Make conscious choices every day that align your actions with your values and dreams; the way you live each day is a sentence in the story of your life. Each day, you choose whether the sentence ends with a period, a question mark, or an exclamation point. Here are ten ideas for writing a life story worth living:

1. Find a passion that makes you come alive.

Don't ask what the world needs. Ask what makes you come alive, and go do it. Because what the world needs, and what every great story has, are characters who have come alive in the pursuit of something that inspires them.

2. Work hard on that passion.

A dream is your creative vision for your life in the future. You must break out of your current comfort zone and become comfortable with the new and unfamiliar. So dream big, pursue your passion, and give yourself permission to work toward a future you know you are capable of creating.

3. Live happily in your own way.

You are not in this world to live up to the expectations of others, nor should you feel that others are here to live up to yours. Pave your own unique path. What success means to each of us is totally different. Ultimately, success is about spending your life happily in your own way.

4. Change your path when you must, but keep moving forward.

There are millions of possible paths one could take up the mountain of life. You get to choose which one you take, and you can jump from one path to another if you run into a roadblock. The only mistake you can make is standing still.

5. When the going gets tough, keep fighting.

The wisest, most loving, most well-rounded people you have met are likely those who have known failure, defeat, and suffering, and have found their way out of the depths of their own despair. These people have gained compassion, understanding, and a deep sense of gratitude. People like this aren't born; they develop slowly over the course of a lifetime.

6. Let go of the past and live consciously in the present.

Life can only be understood backward, but it must be lived forward. The past is a good place to visit on occasion, but not a great place to stay. Don't waste time trying to relive or change your past when you have priceless moments unfolding in front of you right now.

7. Embrace new ideas, lessons, and challenges.

There is nothing more wonderful than seeing life as an adventure. Try things that you're afraid of. Look deeply into the unknown and enjoy it.

Because when you face new challenges, you're learning, growing, and truly living.

8. Appreciate the little things in life that mean a lot.

Think of all the beauty around you, and be happy. Be thankful for all the small things in your life, because when you put them all together you will see just how significant they are. Remember, it's not happiness that makes us grateful, but gratefulness that makes us happy.

9. Live honorably through kindness.

If you live honorably, no matter how old you get, life will always remain beautiful—and so will you. And remember, there is no better exercise for the heart than reaching out and holding the hand of someone in need.

10. Spend quality time with people you love.

Appreciate the people who love and care for you most. Spend time with them. Someday you will either regret not doing so, or you will say, "I'm glad I did."

11 THINGS You FORGET You're Doing Wrong

WHEN YOU STOP doing the wrong things, the right things eventually catch you. So make sure you're not . . .

1. Making blind judgments

Too often we jump to conclusions only to cause ourselves and others unnecessary worry, hurt, and anger. So exercise restraint, be kind, and save the jumping for joy.

2. Expecting people to be perfect

When you open up to love, you must be open to getting hurt as well. When you stop expecting people to be perfect, you can start appreciating them for who they truly are.

3. Focusing on everything and everyone except you

Make the world a better place one person at a time, and start with *you*. If you're looking out into the world to find where your purpose resides, stop—and look inside instead. Look at who you already are, the lifestyle you choose to live, and what makes you come alive. Follow them into the world with courage and newfound purpose.

4. Holding on to the wrong things for too long

To let go isn't to forget. Letting go involves cherishing the memories, overcoming the obstacles, and moving on. It's all about finding the strength to embrace life's changes and continue taking positive steps forward.

5. Denying your mistakes

Mistakes are almost always forgivable if you have the courage to admit them. Sometimes falling flat on your face is exactly what's needed to help you see things from a totally different perspective and get back on track.

6. Avoiding your fears

Approach your fears, sit with them, and really get to know them. Your fears are your friends; their only job is to show you undeveloped parts of yourself that you need to cultivate to live a happy life. The more you do the things you're most afraid of doing, the more life opens up.

7. Accepting less than you know you deserve

Do not sacrifice your heart or your dignity. Love yourself enough to never lower your standards for the wrong reasons. Be willing to walk away, with your head held high.

8. Storing mental clutter

Do some sorting, throw away regrets and old pains, and take only the treasures worth keeping: the lessons, the love, and the best of what you've lived.

9. Worrying about things that can't be changed

One of the happiest moments is when you feel the courage to let go of what you can't change. The past cannot be changed, forgotten, or erased. However, the lessons learned can prepare you for a brighter tomorrow.

10. Letting hope gradually slip away

We can live without a lot of things, but hope isn't one of them. Cultivate hope by latching on to stories of triumph and words that inspire. But most of all, listen to the quiet whisper of your inner strength when it tells you that you will get through this stronger than you were before.

11. Thinking it's too late

Whether you know it or not, the rest of your life is being shaped right now. You can choose to blame your circumstances on fate or bad luck or bad choices, or you can move forward. The rest of your life is being shaped by the goals you chase, the choices you make, and the actions you take. The rest of your life starts right now.

14 RULES for Being You

EMBRACE THAT INDIVIDUAL inside you who has ideas, strengths, and beauty like no one else. Be the person you know yourself to be—the best version of you—on your terms. And above all, be true to *you*—if you cannot put your heart in it, take yourself out of it. Starting today . . .

1. Get your priorities straight.

Twenty years from now it won't really matter what shoes you wore, how your hair looked, or what brand of jeans you bought. What will matter is how you loved, what you learned, and how you applied this knowledge.

2. Take full responsibility for your goals.

If you really want good things in your life to happen, you have to make them happen yourself. You have to make your own future and not think that your destiny is tied to the actions and choices of others.

3. Know your worth.

When someone treats you like you're just one of many options, help them narrow their choice by removing yourself from the equation. It's not pride—it's self-respect. Know your value and what you have to offer, and never settle for anything less than what you deserve.

4. Choose the right perspective.

Perspective is everything. When faced with long checkout lines or traffic jams, you can get frustrated and enraged, or you can spend that time daydreaming, conversing, or watching the clouds. The first choice will raise your blood pressure. The second will raise your consciousness.

5. Don't let your old problems punish your dreams.

The next time you're tempted to rant about a situation that you think ended unfairly, remind yourself of this: you'll never kill off your anger by beating the story to death. So close your mouth, unclench your fists, and redirect your thoughts. When left untended, the anger will slowly wither, and you'll be left to live in peace as you grow toward a better future.

6. Choose the things that truly matter.

Some things just don't matter much. But lifting a person's heart? Now, that matters. Put first things first. The hardest and smartest way to live is choosing what truly matters and pursuing it passionately.

7. Love you.

Let someone love you just the way you are—as flawed as you might be, as unattractive as you sometimes feel, and as unaccomplished as you think you are. Yes, let someone love you despite all of this, and let that someone be *you*.

8. Accept your strengths and weaknesses.

Everyone has their own strengths and weaknesses, and it is only when we accept everything we are, and everything we aren't, that we are able to become who we are capable of being.

9. Stand up for you.

You're here to be *you*, not to be what someone else wants you to be. Look them in the eye and say, "Don't judge me until you know me, don't underestimate me until you challenge me, and don't talk about me until you've talked to me."

10. Learn from others, and move on when you must.

You can't expect to change people. Either you accept who they are, or you start living your life without them. Some people come into your life as blessings; others come into your life as lessons.

11. Be honest in your relationships.

If you're not happy, be honest, and move on if you must. When you're truly in love, being faithful isn't a sacrifice, it's a joy.

12. Get comfortable with being uncomfortable.

Life can change in the blink of an eye. It might feel a little uncomfortable at times, but know that life begins at the end of your comfort zone. So if you're feeling uncomfortable right now, know that the change taking place in your life is not an ending, but a new beginning.

13. Be who you were born to be.

Don't get to the end of your life and find that you lived only the length of it—live the width of it as well. When you are truly comfortable in your own skin, not everyone will like you, but you won't care about it one bit.

14. Never give up on you.

This is your life; shape it, or someone else will. Strength lives not only in the ability to hold on, but in the ability to start over when you must. Keep learning, adapting, and growing. You may not be there yet, but you are closer than you were yesterday.

11 WAYS to Become the PERSON You Love

YOU ARE POWERFUL when you believe in yourself. You are beautiful when your strength and determination shine as you follow your own path. You are unstoppable when you know you can fall down, pick yourself up, and move forward. Here are eleven ways to become the person you love:

1. Stop judging, and appreciate the beauty within you.

When it comes to being compassionate and nonjudgmental, the only challenge greater than learning to walk a mile in someone else's shoes is learning to walk a lifetime comfortably in your own. In every human being there is soul, worth, and beauty—including in yourself.

2. Treat yourself the way you want others to treat you.

Accept yourself! Insecurity is what's ugly, not how you look or seem to others.

3. Care less about who you are to others.

Don't lose *you* in your search for acceptance from the outside. You have nothing to prove to anyone else. Care less about who you are to others and more about who you are to yourself.

4. Know your worth.

We often accept the love we think we deserve. It makes no sense to be second in someone's life, when you know you're good enough to be first in someone else's.

5. Don't rush intimate relationships.

Love is not about sex, going on fancy dates, or showing off. It's about being with a person who makes you happy in a way that no one else can. If you haven't found true love yet, don't settle. There is someone out there who will love you unconditionally—you just haven't found them yet.

6. Let go of those who aren't really there.

There are certain people who aren't meant to fit into your life no matter how much you want them to. Maybe a happy ending doesn't include anyone else right now. Maybe it's just you, picking up the pieces and starting over, freeing yourself for something better in the future. Maybe the happy ending is simply letting go.

7. Forgive yourself and others.

Life begins where your fear and resentment end. When you forgive yourself and others, and stop the inner imprisonment, you free yourself to live with love and purpose—looking forward, not back.

8. Focus on the positive.

Our thoughts are the makers of our moods, the inventors of our dreams, and the creators of our will. That is why we must sort through them carefully and choose to respond only to those that will help us build the life we want, and the outlook we want to hold as we're living it.

9. Believe in the person you are capable of being.

The real purpose of your life is to evolve and grow into the whole person you are capable of being. Change really is always possible—there is no ability that can't be developed with experience. Don't ever let your negative beliefs stand in the way of your own improvement.

10. Work on goals you believe in.

Never put off or give up on a goal that's important to you. Not because you still have tomorrow to start or try again, but because you may not have tomorrow at all. Life is shorter than it sometimes seems. Follow your heart today.

11. Keep looking and moving forward.

Moving on doesn't mean you have forgotten, it means you have accepted what happened in the past and choose to continue living in the present. It doesn't mean giving up, it means you're giving yourself another chance by making a choice to be happy rather than hurt. Through all the challenges you have faced, you can now say, "I survived and I now know better for next time."

In the end, loving yourself is about enjoying your life, trusting your own feelings, taking chances, losing and finding happiness, cherishing the memories, and learning from the past. Sometimes you have to stop worrying, wondering, and doubting. Have faith that things will work out, maybe not exactly how you planned, but just how it's meant to be.

SELF-LOVE QUESTIONS
TO MAKE YOU THINK

If you had a friend who spoke to you in the same way that you sometimes speak to yourself, how LONG would you allow that person to be your *friend*?

Why are YOU *you*?

In one sentence, what do you WISH for your *future* self?

What's something you have that EVERYONE *wants*?

What's something NOBODY could ever *steal* from you?

What has the little VOICE inside your head been *saying* lately?

What makes you FEEL *incomplete*?

What else would you SEE about yourself if you removed the thought that's been troubling you?

What's something NEW you recently learned about *yourself*?

What PROMISE to yourself do you still need to *fulfill*?

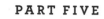

PART FIVE

Passion and Growth

*Be true to YOU. If you cannot put your heart in it,
take yourself out of it.*

I WOULD RATHER
SOUND STUPID

Magic Happens

I've always believed in the beauty of a great journey—discovering new places, seeking life experiences, fostering relationships, and pursuing my dreams. In fact, it's all I've ever really wanted to do. I just want to believe in something that's worth believing in and then pursue it with every facet of my being.

Such journeys, I've found, are best when we share them with others who, like me, are "crazy" enough to assume that our wildest dreams are just a brief distance away from reality. These are the folks who realize that "impossible" is simply a mind-set—something we get when we haven't trained our minds and our hearts to see past the systems that currently exist to ones that don't yet exist. Because when our minds and our hearts and our hands work together, magic happens.

Fear

Only one thing has ever prevented me from making this magic happen more often. Fear. Being afraid of what others might think. Afraid of the repercussions of putting my crazy ideas out there for the world to see and judge. Afraid to let go of my comfort zone and just go for it. Because . . . What if I fail? What if . . . What if . . .

Now, in most situations, fear no longer stands in my way. But that doesn't mean it doesn't exist. It most certainly does. I've just learned to curb my fears and adapt to change a bit more proficiently than I used to. But I still feel the nerves of fear sneak up on me. And the more important something or someone is to me, the more nervous I get, the more I stumble over my words, and the more I sound like an incoherent fool.

A few years ago when I began talking to my friends and family about my goal to write and start the blog that would eventually become *Marc and Angel Hack Life*, I mostly got half smiles, nods, and quizzical facial reactions. And when I tried to say anything meaningful to Angel when we first met back in September of 2000, she would often laugh at me because she literally found herself trying to decode my jumbled, shaky sentences.

Clarity

One of the most remarkable things about our lives is that clarity and progression occur with enduring love, passion, and patience. This book is now an easy topic for me to talk about . . . and now it's even easy for others to talk about, including my friends and family. And although it may take her a second or two, Angel now gets the gist of my jumbled, shaky sentences almost immediately.

And that makes me smile. Because I want to continue to evolve and grow with the people and dreams that inspire me. After all, I only have one shot—like we all do—to make this life meaningful. And I know for sure, after coping with my fears on numerous journeys, that I would rather sound stupid . . . than be stupid and take no action at all.

31 MORNING Journal PROMPTS That Will Change the Way YOU THINK

THE MORNING IS enormously important. It's the foundation on which the day is built. How we choose to spend our mornings can be used to predict the kinds of days we're going to have.

When I wake up in the morning, my mind gradually gathers, and I begin to move as the early-morning light is just starting to seep through the windows. My family is still sleeping. It's a peaceful beginning.

I stretch, drink a glass of water, start the teakettle, and practice a short journaling exercise for ten minutes. Then I enjoy a cup of tea as I read one chapter of a good book. And finally, I write on my laptop, diligently (disconnected from online distractions), for an hour before the hustle of the day begins.

Once my family awakens, I pause to join them for a short time and we appreciate the full presence of each other's company.

This is just a rough sketch of my mornings, and they make me happy.

It wasn't always this way, however. I used to wake up in a hurry, rushing and cranky before stumbling into work and errands and meetings. It was unpleasant, but it was my life. I didn't know any better, so I didn't think I could change. Thankfully, I was wrong.

I've changed my mornings so they work for me and not against me. And although the various changes happened gradually, they all started with one simple, month-long ritual. This ritual gave me the gift of self-reflection at a pivotal point in my life, and it provided me with a solid foundation for making decisions that ultimately altered my thinking on just about everything. I've shared this part of my journey—this ritual—with thousands of course students and conference attendees over the years, and as simple as it is, many of them come back to me a month or so later and say "Thank you!" I'm hoping you find value in it as well.

A Month of Morning Journaling

Journaling is a priceless tool for self-reflection and self-improvement.

J. K. Rowling keeps a journal. Eminem keeps a journal. Oprah keeps a journal. Successful people all over the world—those who consistently make positive changes in their lives—reflect daily and learn from their life experiences. And they often use some kind of journal to accomplish this. For the longest time, I knew the value of journaling—I heard the success stories of others—and yet I never took action. Why? Because I thought I didn't have enough time for it. I was "too busy." That was until my ongoing negligence led to heightened levels of stress that literally put me in a hospital (my life was so disorganized and hectic, I started having panic attacks). I learned the hard way, but *you* don't have to.

If you want to get somewhere in life, you need a map, and your journal is that map. You can write down what you did today, what you tried to accomplish, where you made mistakes, and so much more. It's a place to reflect. It's a place to capture important thoughts. It's a place to sort out where you've been and where you intend to go. And it's one of the most underused yet incredibly effective tools available to the masses.

If you're interested in getting started with journaling, or if you'd like some fresh ideas for your current journaling practice, here are thirty-one journaling prompts below that Angel and I have personally used in the past to nudge ourselves into self-reflection. They will bring awareness to the unconscious beliefs and assumptions you have. And they will help you think through situations, big and small, and make better decisions.

Challenge yourself to read and write on each prompt for at least five minutes every morning for the next month. See how doing so gradually changes your life.

Day 1

Forgive yourself for the bad decisions you made, for the times you lacked understanding, for the choices that hurt others and yourself. Forgive yourself for being young and reckless. These are all vital lessons. And what matters most right now is your willingness to grow from them.

What specifically do you need to forgive yourself for? What have your error(s) in judgment taught you?

Day 2

The mind is your battleground. It's the place where the fiercest conflict resides. It's where half the things you feared would happen never actually happened. It's where your expectations get the best of you, and where you fall victim to your own train of thought time and time again.

What's one thought that has been getting the best of you lately? How has it been influencing your behavior?

Day 3

What you focus on grows. Stop managing your time. Start managing your focus. Bring your attention back to what's important.

What is truly worth focusing on today? What is *not*?

Day 4

Happiness is letting go of what you assume your life is supposed to be like right now, and sincerely appreciating it for everything that it is. So, *relax*. You are enough. You have enough. You do enough. Breathe deep . . . let go, and just live right now in the moment.

What do you appreciate most about your life right now? Why?

Day 5

A tiny part of your life is decided by uncontrollable circumstances, while the vast majority of it is decided by your internal responses. Let this sink in. Regardless of what's going on around you, peace of mind arrives the moment you make peace with what's on your mind.

What is one reality you need to make peace with? Why?

Day 6

As we mentioned in the introduction, it's funny how we outgrow what we once thought we couldn't live without, and then we fall in love with what we didn't even know we wanted. Life keeps leading us on journeys we would never go on if it were up to us. Don't be afraid. Have faith. Find the lessons. Trust the journey.

What's something you've let go that once meant the world to you? And what's something you love today that you never even knew you needed in your life?

Day 7

Most of the time you have a choice. If you don't like a changeable aspect of your life, it's time to start making changes and new choices. And it's OK to be low-key about it. You don't need to put everything on social media. Silently progress and let your actions speak for themselves.

Over the past month, what have your actions been silently saying about your priorities? Are there any changes you want to make? If so, elaborate.

Day 8

We waste our time waiting for the ideal path to appear. But it never does. Because we forget that paths are made by walking, not waiting. And no, you shouldn't feel more confident before you take the next step. Taking the next step is what builds your confidence.

What's the next step you've been thinking about taking—for far too long?

Day 9

The next step means nothing if you are in love with your comfort zone and simply walking in circles. Don't live the same day thirty thousand times and call it a life! Growth begins today, at the end of your comfort zone. Dream. Attempt. Explore. This moment is the doorway to anything you want.

How have you stretched your comfort zone in the past month (even slightly)? What did you learn from this experience? What's one new comfort zone challenge you'd like to conquer?

Day 10

Your capacity to be happy is directly related to the quality of people who most closely surround you. So be with those who are good for your mental health. Those who bring you inner peace. Those who challenge your bad habits but also support your ability to change and grow.

Whom have you spent the most time with over the past month, and how have these people affected your life?

Day 11

Too often we say "life is not fair" while we're eating our food, sipping a drink, and reading tweets on our smartphones. Think twice, and be thankful. At the end of the day, before you close your eyes, breathe deeply, appreciate where you are, and see the value in what you have.

What is one privilege you have that you often take for granted?

Day 12

When things aren't adding up in your life, begin subtracting. Life gets a lot simpler when you clear the clutter that makes it complicated. Fill your life with lots of experiences, not lots of things. Have incredible stories to tell, not incredible clutter in your closets.

What kinds of physical clutter have been complicating your life and diverting you from meaningful life experiences?

Day 13

Even when it seems personal, rarely do people do things because of you, they do things because of them. You know this is true. You may not be able to control all the things people say and do to you, but you can decide not to be reduced by them. Make that decision for yourself today.

What's something you often take too personally even though, logically, you know better? How has this habit affected your life?

Day 14

You can't control how other people receive your energy. Anything you do or say gets filtered through the lens of whatever they are going through at the moment, which has nothing to do with you. Just keep doing your thing with as much love and integrity as possible.

What's one good, recent example of someone with a bad attitude completely misjudging you?

Day 15

You won't always be a priority to others, and that's why you have to be a priority to yourself. Learn to respect yourself, take care of yourself, and become your own support system. Your needs matter. Start meeting them. Don't wait on others to choose you. Choose yourself, today!

How have you chosen yourself recently? How will you choose yourself today?

Day 16

Just breathe, be, and pay attention to what it's like to be *you*. Nothing to fix. Nothing to change. Nowhere else to go. Just you, breathing, being, with presence, without judgment. You are welcome here. You belong here. Here, you are enough. Close your eyes. Breathe . . .

What's something true about you that you need to embrace more openly and lovingly?

Day 17

The wisest, most loving, and most well-rounded people you have ever met are likely those who have been shattered by heartbreak. Yes, life creates the best humans by breaking them first. Their destruction into pieces allows them to be fine-tuned and reconstructed into a masterpiece.

How has your past heartbreak made you stronger, wiser, and more loving? Be specific.

Day 18

There's a big difference between giving up and starting over in the right direction. Know when enough is enough already, and respect yourself for feeling that way. Sometimes we have to say good-bye before we can say hello. Sometimes we have to let go to move forward with our lives.

What's something from your past that you are thankful you gave up on? Why?

Day 19

Give yourself the space to hear your own voice—your own soul. Too many of us listen to the noise of the world and get lost in the crowd. Stand strong! Live by choice, not by chance. Work to grow, not compete. Choose to listen to yourself, not the jumbled opinions of everyone else.

What has your inner voice been trying to tell you lately? What does it mean?

Day 20

Forget popularity. Just do your thing with passion, humility, and honesty. Do what you do, not for an applause, but because it's what's right. Pursue it a little bit each day, no matter what anyone else thinks. That's how dreams are achieved.

What's something that's worth working on today, regardless of what other people think? Why is it so important to you?

Day 21

If it entertains you now but will hurt or bore you someday, it's a distraction. Don't settle. Don't exchange what you want most for what you kind of want at the moment. Study your habits. Figure out where your time goes, and remove distractions. It's time to focus on what matters.

What distractions have been getting the best of you lately? How often? Why?

Day 22

Don't fall back into your old patterns of living just because they're more comfortable and easier to access. Remember, you left certain habits and situations behind for a reason: to improve your life. And right now, you can't move forward if you keep going back.

What's one old pattern of behavior that sometimes still sneaks up on you? What's a better alternative, and why?

Day 23

Your mind and body need to be exercised to gain strength. They need to be challenged consistently. If you haven't pushed yourself in lots of little ways over time—if you always avoid doing the hard things—you'll crumble on the inevitable days that are harder than you expected.

How can you provide healthy challenges for both your mind and body on a daily basis? What will you do today to walk the talk?

Day 24

As you age, you'll learn to value your time, genuine relationships, meaningful work, and peace of mind much more. Little else will matter. Thus, the strongest sign of your growth is realizing you're no longer worried or stressed by the trivial things that once used to drain you.

What's something that used to drive you crazy but no longer bothers you? Why?

Day 25

Remind yourself that everyone you meet is afraid of something, loves something, and has lost something. Respect this. And be extra kind. Take time to really listen. Take time to learn something new. Take time to say thank you. Today.

What can you easily do to be a little kinder than usual today? And who was the last person who was unexpectedly kind to you?

Day 26

People will rarely think and act exactly the way you want them to. Hope for the best, but expect less. Agree to disagree when necessary. And be careful not to dehumanize those you disagree with. In our self-righteousness, we can easily become the very things we dislike in others.

How have your recent expectations of others gotten the best of you? What happened, and what have you learned?

Day 27

Love what you do, until you can do what you love. Love where you are, until you can be where you love. Love the people you are with, until you can be with the people you love most. This is the way we find happiness, opportunity, and peace.

How will you embody "love" today? What specifically will you do?

Day 28

The older we grow, the more peaceful we become. Life humbles us gradually as we age. We realize how much nonsense we've wasted time on. So just do your best right now to feel the peace that flows from your decision to rise above the petty drama that doesn't really matter.

What kind of drama do you sometimes get caught up in? What can you do to rise above it?

Day 29

It's not too late. You aren't behind. You're exactly where you need to be. Every step is necessary. Don't judge or berate yourself for how long your journey is taking. We all need our own time to travel our own distance. Give yourself credit. And be thankful you made it this far.

How far have you come? How much have you grown? Think about the specifics of your recent and long-term growth. What have you not given yourself enough credit for?

Day 30

You're not the same person you were a year ago, a month ago, or a week ago. You're always growing. Experiences don't stop. That's life. And the very experiences that seem so hard when you're going through them are the ones you'll look back on with gratitude for how far you've come.

What's the hardest thing you're trying to accomplish or cope with right now? What is something small but necessary about this struggle?

Day 31

There will come a time when you think it's all over, everything is finished . . . you've reached the end of the road. That's the starting line. Be humble. Be teachable. The world is bigger than your view of it. There's always room for a new idea, a new step . . . a new beginning.

What does a new beginning mean to you right now? What is the first thing you will do with it?

Consistency Is Everything

These morning journaling prompts mean almost nothing if they are not practiced consistently. One morning of journaling by itself won't cut it. It is the compound effect of simple, seemingly mundane actions over time that leads to life-altering, positive results.

There is nothing immediately exciting about putting one foot in front of the other every day for weeks, but by doing so, many normal human beings have climbed more than 29,000 feet to the top of the highest mountain in the world, Mount Everest.

You have a choice! Choose to put one foot in front of the other from the get-go, when it would be easier not to. Choose to open your journal at dawn, when it would be easier to sleep in. Prove to yourself, in little ways every morning, that you have the power to take control of your day, and your life.

18 THINGS My DAD Was Right About

TWENTY-FIVE YEARS AGO, when I was a freshman in high school, my English teacher gave my class a homework assignment entitled "Advice for a Younger Generation." The concept of the assignment was simple: Each student had to interview a person who was over the age of twenty-five, gather enough information to write a basic biography of their life, and find out what their top tips were for a younger generation. I chose to interview my dad. He was fifty-three at the time and he gave me eighteen pieces of advice.

I had completely forgotten about all this until recently, when I was visiting my parents and was cleaning out a few old boxes in the attic. In one of these boxes I found the original "Advice for a Younger Generation" assignment, dated April 22, 1996. I read through it and was totally blown away.

Even though my dad's advice is relevant to a person of any age, my adult self can relate to it in a way my fourteen-year-old self didn't quite grasp at the time. In fact, the first thought I had when reading this list was, "My dad was right."

Here are his eighteen pieces of advice for a younger generation, transcribed with his permission:

1. Your thirties, forties, and fifties won't feel like your thirties, forties, and fifties.

Adults are just older children. For the most part, you still feel exactly the way you feel right now, just a little wiser and more confident. You've had time to establish your place in the world and figure out what's important to you. Don't fear growing up. Look forward to it. It's awesome.

2. Bad things will happen to you and your friends.

Part of living and growing up is experiencing unexpected troubles in life. Remember that tragedies are rarely as bad as they seem, and even when they are, they give us an opportunity to grow stronger.

3. Everyone can make a huge difference.

It's easy to feel small and hopeless. But every kind gesture lifts the spirit, and the choices we make every day matter—to ourselves and those around us.

4. First impressions aren't all they're cracked up to be.

Everyone and everything seems normal from a distance, or at a glance. The tenth, twentieth, or even the fiftieth impression is when you start to truly understand someone else for who they truly are.

5. Big results come when you narrow your focus.

Concentrate your efforts on smaller and smaller areas. When your efforts are diffused over a wide area, they won't have much of an impact. Think small, and the effects will be large.

6. Love yourself. Become your own priority.

Strive to be the "you" you want to be. Nourish your mind and body. Educate yourself every day until you die.

7. Sometimes you just have to go for it.

People rarely get it right the first time. In fact, usually the only people who ever get it right are those who continue going for it even when they've come up short numerous times before.

8. In order to get, you have to give.

Supporting, guiding, and making contributions to other people is one of life's greatest rewards. Everything you do comes back around.

9. Not much is worth fighting about.

Don't let a single poisonous moment of misunderstanding make you forget about the countless loving moments you've spent together. If you're angry at someone you love, hug them and mean it. You may not feel like hugging them, which is all the more reason to do so.

10. Don't try to impress everyone.

Be real with people instead. Connect with fewer people on a level that is deeper and more profound.

11. Keep having fun.

Fun can seem like an indulgence. It should be a requirement. Make time for fun.

12. Keep it simple.

Pick the five most important things in your life now and focus on those things. Let the other stuff go. Stop the busyness and really enjoy what's important to you.

13. Little things stick with you.

So pay attention to them. Like watching your child sleep. Preparing a meal with your family. Sharing a great laugh with an old friend. This is the real stuff life is made of.

14. Keep your opinions to yourself.

Be a sounding board, not a stage director. The people in your life will thank you—and find their own path.

15. Manage your time.

Be careful not to confuse things that are urgent with things that are important.

16. Manage your money.

Don't let your money manage you.

17. What you learn in school does matter.

While you may not use the specifics of every classroom lesson, over time you will develop problem-solving skills that are universally applicable.

18. Dreams will remain dreams forever if you don't take action.

Don't dream about it anymore. Start doing it. Forty years from now, what is it that you will regret not having accomplished, appreciated, or attempted? Do it, appreciate it, and attempt it *now*!

10 LIES You Will HEAR Before You Pursue Your Dreams

UNFORTUNATELY, JUST BEFORE you take your first step on the righteous journey to pursue your dreams, people around you, even the ones who deeply care for you, will give you awful advice. It's not because they have evil intentions. It's because they don't understand the big picture—what your dreams, passions, and life goals mean to you. They don't understand that, to you, the reward is worth the risk.

So they try to protect you by shielding you from the possibility of failure, which, in effect, also shields you from the possibility of making your dreams a reality.

Here are ten ill-advised tips (lies) people will likely tell you when you decide to pursue your dreams, and why they are dreadfully mistaken.

1. You can follow your dreams someday, but right now you need to buckle down and be responsible.

When is "someday"? It's a foggy generalization of a time that will likely never come. Today is the only day you can begin to make a difference in your life. And pursuing your dreams is what life is all about. Don't wait until "someday." Make today the first day of the rest of your new life.

2. You're totally screwed if it doesn't work out.

Wrong! In fact, the worst-case scenario is that things don't work out and you have to go back to doing exactly what you are doing right now.

3. It's safer to stay at your day job.

Avoiding risks can be the riskiest path of all. Remember, safer doesn't always mean better.

4. That's impossible!

It's only impossible if you never do anything about it. If you truly dedicate yourself to an end result, almost anything is possible. You just have to want it badly enough.

5. Only a lucky few "make it."

That's because those lucky few did something about it! They had the drive, determination, and willpower that you have right now. You can be one of them. It's up to you, and only you.

6. You might fail. And failing is bad.

Failures are simply stepping-stones to success. Either you succeed or you learn something. Win–win. The biggest mistake you can make is doing nothing because you're too scared to make a mistake.

7. You will sacrifice too much for too little.

When it comes to working hard to achieve a dream—earning a degree, building a business, or any other personal achievement that takes time and commitment—one thing you have to ask yourself is: "Am I willing to live a few years of my life like many people won't, so I can spend the rest of my life like many people can't?"

8. You need more money saved before you can take the first step.

You don't need more money. You need a plan. Studying those who have succeeded with similar ventures can help. But above all, take baby steps. Don't be foolish and assume that you must have a certain amount of money saved right now, or that you must quit your day job today in order to pursue your dreams. Instead, ask yourself, "What actions can I take right now with the money and resources I have right now that will bring me closer to my desired goal?"

9. You don't need any help. It's smarter to go after it alone.

Surrounding yourself with positive people will increase your effectiveness and your chances for success. So spend time with people who support your goals. If you are around cynical and negative people all the time, you will become cynical and negative. Is who you are and who you want to be reflected in the company you keep?

10. That sounds like a lot of hard work.

You're darn right it does! But that doesn't mean it's not worth it. We think success in life hinges on one key point: finding hard work you love doing. As long as you remain true to yourself and follow your own interests, values, and dreams, you can find success through passion. Perhaps most important, you won't wake up a few years from now working in a field you despise, wondering, "How the heck am I going to do this for the next thirty years?" So if you catch yourself working hard and loving every minute of it, don't stop. You're onto something big. Disregard these misguided bits of nonsense and you'll be well on your way to fulfilling your dreams.

Now get out there and make a splash!

8 REASONS to STOP Waiting for APPROVAL

ONE OF THE greatest freedoms is simply not caring what everyone else thinks of you. Don't just accept the safe and easy choices because you're afraid of what others will think, or afraid of what might happen. If you do, nothing will ever happen. Don't let small minds convince you that your dreams are too big. Starting today, stop waiting for approval. Here's why:

1. You only get one life to pursue the dreams that make you come alive.

It is better to be failing (and learning) at doing something you love, rather than succeeding at doing something you hate. So take chances on behalf of what you believe in. Fail until you succeed. Face your fears with courage and passion. Keep your word and hold true to your vision until it comes to life.

2. Someone else's approval is just another opinion.

Never sacrifice who you are, or who you aspire to be, because someone else has a problem with it. Love who you are inside and out, and keep pushing forward. No one else has the power to make you feel small unless you give them that power. You are the only one who can create your dreams and happiness.

3. The only opinion of you that really matters is your own.

Give up on the desire to be perfect in the eyes of others, and begin the journey of becoming your true self. What you love determines your dreams, your dreams determine your actions, and your actions determine your destiny.

4. Some people will never give you their approval anyway.

There are two kinds of people—those who are a drain on your energy and creative force, and those who give you energy and support your creativity, even with the simplest gesture, like a smile. Avoid the first kind. Be who you want to be. If others don't like it, let them be. Happiness is a choice—*your* choice.

5. Everyone's journey and perspective on life is different.

Do not change your unique foundation for anyone. What lies ahead will always be a bit of a mystery. Do not be afraid to explore, learn, and grow. Why some things happen will never be certain. Take it in stride and move forward.

6. Firsthand experience is often necessary for personal growth.

Some life lessons can only be understood by going through them on your own. This experience gives you the ability to think more logically and take educated steps in a positive direction.

7. Your intuition requires no approval.

When it comes to exercising your inner genius, you must try what you want to try, go where you want to go, and follow your own intuition. Don't let others put a cage around your ideas. If it feels right, take a chance. Because you never know how remarkable it could turn out to be.

8. Life is too short to wait any longer.

In the grand scheme of things, you don't have much time left—no one does. So look around at this gift you've been given and choose to be happy, without approval. What have you got to lose?

YOU CAN CHANGE
THE WORLD

An Epiphany

Imagine for a moment the year is 2000 B.C.E. and you're a fisherman living along the coast of what is now Southern Europe. Like any other morning, you're fishing when suddenly a powerful burst of energy enters your body. It creates a tingling sensation in your fingertips, a flutter in your heart, and warmth in your belly. You know it's not anxiety or a heart attack because it feels comforting and fulfilling.

You put your fishing pole down and sit at the water's edge. You reach down and splash a handful of cool water up onto your face. It is here, in this quiet moment, that you have an epiphany. And while you are unable to explain how or why this epiphany is coming to you now—you haven't done anything out of the ordinary to receive it—its message is crystal clear:

The Earth is not flat. The Earth is a sphere. You can visualize it revolving around the sun in a predictable orbital pattern. These visualizations also reveal that the Earth is part of a solar system of eight planets separate from stars in the night's sky and that these other stars follow similar predictable patterns of movement. There is a whole uncharted universe out there that nobody else is aware of.

Once the magnitude of your epiphany settles in your mind, you begin to sweat from nervousness. Because while the small seaside village you live in is peaceful, there is little tolerance for outlandish ideas and theories like the ones that just rattled your brain. If you were to tell others about them, the nobles and town leaders might interpret it as a direct threat to the cultural stability of the community, and the rest of the villagers would likely think you're crazy. You could be exiled!

You decide that you must handle your business as usual and leave the deep visions and epiphanies to the witch doctors and nomads who dwell in the forests on the outskirts of civilization. These people have already decided that the world they grew up in doesn't hold the answers they are looking for. They are the ones who should convey these outlandish ideas to the world. Because they have nothing to lose. At least not as much as you do.

So, you don't tell a soul about your epiphany. Days roll into weeks. Weeks roll into months. And you imagine, each day, that you are better off for having kept it a secret. But you are also aware that keeping this secret is eating away at you from the inside out. You have distanced yourself from people and have been sleeping less and less. Your mind won't stop stirring.

Words of Wisdom

One night, after hours of stirring, you finally fall asleep and begin to dream. You dream you're sitting at a round table in a dimly lit room. There is a woman sitting across the table from you. You can barely make out her face, but you can see her hair is silver and her skin is worn. She seems old and wise. And it feels like she can see right through to your soul. But you also feel comforted because there is nothing to hide from her. She already knows what you know.

"Do you know why you're sitting here with me?" she asks in a low, soothing voice.

"I don't know," you reply. "I guess I'm here because I have no one else I can talk to."

She smiles and says, "You are here because you have something to say. Something you know is of immense importance; it's something that will change the world when you finally say it. But you are afraid to say it because you don't think people are ready to hear it."

You sit in silence with her for a moment, just staring into her eyes. You feel an energy emanating from her heart that gently soothes yours. Easing it of tension. Letting it know that it can beat loudly and proudly at any pace it wants to without concern. Because it's safe here—a sanctuary devoid of judgment. And all of the fear inside you slowly subsides.

You take a deep breath and say, "I am here because I had an epiphany in which I saw, clearly, that the Earth is not flat. It is a sphere that revolves around the sun as part of an eight-planet solar system. And there are other stars out there too, perhaps in other solar systems in what is likely a vast, uncharted universe."

You pause for a moment, take two more deep breaths, and continue, "I don't know where this epiphany came from or why it came to me when it did. But I've since done some preliminary tests and the results seem to prove my epiphany's accuracy. In fact, at this point I'm certain it's accurate. And I'm certain, also, that the people of this world aren't ready for it. I have already been punished for having this epiphany—for simply knowing what I know. And I don't want to be punished once more for conveying what I know to others."

She smiles again. And, as she smiles, you feel more comforted than you have since before you had your epiphany. "In all walks of life, you will never know when the world is ready," she says. "You will only know when you are ready. And you will know when you are simply because you will take action and do something about it. And after you do something, you will know when there is more to do, because you will do more."

Her words of wisdom are so clear, so simple. But the real world, you recall, is far more twisted and convoluted. In the real world, there are cultures and customs that have been around for generations that must be dealt with.

"The most important thing to remember," she continues, "is that while it may feel like you are at the mercy of the world, you are not. Because the world around you is merely a reflection of what's inside you—your thoughts. So what feels like an entire world that isn't ready, isn't really a world at all. It's just you. And when you change, you will notice that the world outside has changed too."

You Have Changed

Your eyes slowly open. You sit up in bed and silently meditate on your dream. After a few moments, you stand up and walk out the front door of your cabin to get some fresh air. And as you stand there watching the sun rise over the village, you notice something is different. The entire village seems brighter and more alive than you remember. Has the village changed? Have the people changed? Or is it just you? You aren't sure.

What you are sure of is that you have fish to catch today. And that you have something important to say. And while you don't know yet how you will say it, you are gradually growing more and more confident that you will know soon. And by the time you realize you know, you will have already begun to say what you need to say.

And the world around you will have already begun to change.

Because you have changed.

10 THINGS to DO Even If They Judge You

WHAT WOULD YOU do differently if you knew nobody would judge you? People may have heard your stories, but they aren't living your life. So forget what they say. Focus on how you feel, and do what you know in your heart is right. Here are ten things to do even if others judge you for it:

1. Take care of yourself.

If you don't take good care of yourself, then you can't take good care of others either—which is why taking care of yourself is the best selfish thing you can do.

2. Do what you know is right for you.

Don't let anyone's ignorance, drama, or negativity stop you from being the best you can be. Because when you are totally at peace within yourself, nothing can shake you.

3. Follow your own unique path.

Every new day is a chance to change your life. Work on making life all that you want it to be. And while you're out there making decisions instead of excuses, learning new things, and getting closer and closer to your goals, know that there are others out there, like us, who admire your efforts and are striving for greatness too.

4. Focus every day on reaching your goals.

The way we spend our time defines who we are. Successful people keep moving by doing small things every day that bring them a couple steps closer to their dream. They make mistakes along the way, but they don't quit—they learn and press on.

5. Adjust your goals and dreams as life changes.

Life is unpredictable, but it provides plenty of opportunities to make dreams come true. Just don't forget that sometimes taking a positive step forward requires you to slightly adjust your dreams, or plan new ones—it's OK to change your mind and change course if you need to.

6. Forgive those who have wronged you.

Forgiveness is a gift you give yourself. It allows you to focus on the future without combating the past. Without forgiveness, wounds can never be healed, and moving on can never be accomplished. What happened in the past is just one chapter. Don't close the book, just turn the page.

7. Show everyone your love and kindness.

If you are reserving your love only for those who you have decided are worthy of it—strangers excluded—it may come as a surprise to learn that this is not love at all, it is called "judgment." Just as the sunlight and the wind do not discriminate, true love does not make any such distinctions either. Love and kindness are ways of living. Where there is love, there is no judgment. Where there is judgment, there is no love.

8. Stand up for others, even if it's the unpopular thing to do.

Sometimes you will say something really small and simple, but it will fit right into an empty space in someone's heart. Dare to reach into the darkness, to pull someone else into the light. Remember, strong people stand up for themselves, but stronger people stand up for others too, and lend a hand when they're able.

9. Fight through your failures.

When you are feeling down or dealing with setbacks, don't be ashamed. You are going through a difficult time, and you are still pushing forward. That's something to be proud of—that you are fighting through it and slowly rising above it. Know that today you are a lot stronger than you were yesterday, and you will continue to be.

10. Keep your head held high and keep smiling.

Don't cry over the past, cry to get over the past. Don't smile to hide the pain, smile to heal the pain. Don't think of all the sadness in the world, think of all the beauty that still remains around you.

15 WAYS to LIVE, and Not Merely Exist

FAR TOO OFTEN we travel through life on autopilot, going through the motions, accepting what is, and having every day pass like the one before it. Everything seems relatively normal and comfortable, except that twitch in the back of your mind that's saying, "It's time to make some changes."

Here are fifteen simple suggestions for those who want to break free from the mold and truly live more of their life—to experience it and enjoy it to the fullest instead of settling for a mere existence.

1. Appreciate the great people and things in your life.

Sometimes we don't notice the things others do for us until they stop doing them. Be grateful for what you have, who loves you, and who cares for you. Truly appreciate life, and you'll find that you have more of it to live.

2. Tune out other people's negativity.

Ignore unconstructive, hurtful commentary. No one has the right to judge you. You alone can deny their poisonous words access to your heart and mind.

3. Forgive those who have hurt you.

The first to apologize is the bravest. The first to forgive is the strongest. The first to move forward is the happiest. Be brave. Be strong. Be happy. Be free.

4. Be who you really are.

In this world that's trying to make you like everyone else, find the courage to keep being your awesome self. And when they laugh at you for being different, laugh back at them for being the same. It takes a lot of courage to stand alone, but it's worth it. Being *you* is worth it!

5. Choose to listen to your inner voice.

Life is a courageous journey or nothing at all. It's your road, and yours alone. Others may walk it with you, but no one can walk it for you.

6. Embrace change and enjoy your life as it unfolds.

The hardest part about growing is letting go of what you were used to, and moving on with something you're not. You might not end up exactly where you intended to go, but eventually you will arrive precisely where you need to be.

7. Choose your relationships wisely.

The best relationships are not just about the good times you share, they're also about the obstacles you go through together, and the fact that you still say "I love you" in the end. Don't let loneliness drive you back into the arms of someone you know you don't belong with. A great relationship is worth waiting for.

8. Recognize those who love you.

The most memorable people in your life will be the ones who loved you when you weren't very lovable. Pay attention to who these people are in your life and love them back, even when they aren't acting lovable themselves.

9. Love yourself too.

If you can love children, in spite of the messes they make; your mother, in spite of her tendency to nag; your father, even though he's too opinionated; your sibling, even though she's always late; your friend, even though he often forgets to return what he borrows, then you know how to love imperfect people, and can surely love yourself.

10. Do things your future self will thank you for.

What you do every day matters more than what you do every once in a while. What you do today is important because you are exchanging a day of your life for it. Make sure it's worthwhile.

11. Be thankful for all the troubles you don't have.

There are two ways of being rich: one is to have all you want, the other is to be satisfied with what you have. Accept and appreciate things now, and you'll find more happiness in every moment you live. And remember, you have to fight through some bad days to earn the best days of your life.

12. Leave enough time for fun.

Sometimes you need to take a few steps back to see things clearly. Never let your life become so filled with work, your mind become so crammed with worry, or your heart become so jammed with old hurts or anger, that there's no room left in them for fun.

13. Enjoy the little things in life.

There is joy and wonder to be had in the simplest of moments: watching the sun set over the horizon or spending time with a family member. Enjoy the little things, because one day you may look back and discover they were the big things.

14. Accept the fact that the past is not today.

Don't let the past steal your present and future from you. We all make mistakes, have struggles, and even regret things in our past. But you are not your mistakes, you are not your struggles, and you are here *now* with the power to shape your day and your future.

15. Let go when you must.

It's not always about trying to fix something that's broken. Some relationships and situations just can't be fixed. If you try to force them back together, things will only get worse. Sometimes it's about starting over and creating something better. Strength shows not only in the ability to persist, but in the ability to start over again with a smile on your face and passion in your heart.

PASSION QUESTIONS TO MAKE YOU THINK

What will you NEVER *give up* on?

What activities make you LOSE track of *time*?

What FASCINATES *you*?

What's SOMETHING you would do *every day* if you could?

At what time in your recent past have you felt most PASSIONATE and *alive*?

Are you doing what you BELIEVE in, or are you *settling* for what you are doing?

What ONE thing have you not done that you really want to do? What's *holding* you back?

What is something you would HATE to go *without* for a day?

Would you rather have LESS work to do, or *more* work you actually enjoy doing?

What would you do DIFFERENTLY if you knew nobody would *judge* you?

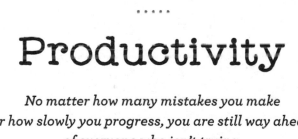

PART SIX

·····

Productivity

No matter how many mistakes you make
or how slowly you progress, you are still way ahead
of everyone who isn't trying.

LESS THAN PERFECT IS A PERFECT START

Her First Subscriber

"How did you do it?" she asked. "In a sea of blogs that never make it, how did you start a personal blog that attracted the attention of ten thousand subscribers?"

I chuckled. "You know, I've been trying to wrap my mind around that one myself."

"Come on, Marc," she insisted. "I'm being serious here. I'm getting ready to start my own blog and I'm nervous about failing. I want to cross all my *t*'s and dot all my *i*'s—I don't want to start it until I know how to do it right."

I stared at her for a moment. "Well, one Sunday evening a few years ago, I made a decision to write an article about something that inspired me, and then I published it on my blog. And every Sunday evening since, I've made a similar decision."

"That's it?" she asked. "No launch plan? No design tweaks? No marketing?"

"No, at least not initially," I replied. "I did a little tweaking down the road, but by then my blog already had a catalog of articles up online.

And most of the tweaks were based on reader feedback and analyzing visitor stats to see which articles were attracting the most attention."

"So you think I simply need to start writing, right now . . . about the things that inspire me?"

"Yeah," I replied. "The only way you can fail is by not writing—by waiting around until you have the perfect plan before you start. Because 'perfect' doesn't exist. It isn't human. It isn't you."

She smiled and said, "Thank you."

Later that afternoon, she e-mailed me a link to her first published blog article. And I became her first subscriber.

What's the Core Purpose?

The hardest part, we have found, of creating something new—a website, a product, a technology—is simply the act of starting. We let our creative minds get so caught up in planning and designing idealistic requirements and prerequisites for our new creation that we drastically hinder the actual process of creating it.

What stops most people from starting with a less-than-perfect plan or product is the fear of failure. There's a common misconception that if you don't get it done exactly right the first time, your creation will fail and all efforts will be lost. That without this feature or that tweak, there's no point at all. Nonsense.

The truth is every successful creation or innovation has a foundational core purpose—a tiny essence that justifies its existence. Any tweak or feature above and beyond the scope of this core purpose is optional. When my friend decided she wanted to start a blog, she spent all of her energy mapping out the perfect plan and design, instead of simply writing her first few blog articles—which is the core purpose of a blog.

So the next time you decide to create something new, back yourself into a corner, cut out the fluff, and release your core creation into the wild ASAP for others to experience. Less than perfect is a perfect start. The need for intelligent tweaks and adjustments will arise naturally as time rolls on.

20 THINGS That Will Matter a Lot LESS to You in 20 YEARS

Too often we let the little frustrations of each day blind us to the beauty in front of us. We get caught up in our own heads and don't know our lives to be any better than the few things that aren't going our way. We call people to complain or spew our gripes on social media. "Life is so unfair!" we yell. And everyone agrees and throws their two cents into the gossip pool.

Other times we talk a big talk about a lot of stuff that really doesn't matter that much. We scrutinize and dramatize the insignificant until we're blue in the face, and then we sit back and scratch our heads in bewilderment about how unfulfilling life feels.

But the older we grow, the quieter we become and the less pointless drama and chaos we engage in. Life humbles us gradually as we age. We realize how much nonsense we've wasted time on. Here are twenty things we eventually realize matter a lot less than we originally thought:

1. The inevitable frustrations of an average day. Ninety-nine percent of what's stressing you out today won't matter a month from now.

Sooner or later you will know this for certain. So do your best to let go of the nonsense, stay positive, and move forward with your life.

2. The little failures you often feel self-conscious about. When you set goals and take calculated risks in life, you eventually learn that there will be times when you succeed and times when you fail, and both are equally important in the long run.

3. How "perfect" everything could be, or should be. Understanding the difference between reasonable striving and perfectionism is critical to picking up your life. Perfectionism not only causes you unnecessary stress and anxiety from the superficial need to always "get it right," it actually prevents you from getting anything worthwhile done at all.

4. Having complete confidence before taking the first step. Confidence is that inner momentum that propels us to bypass our empty fears and self-doubts. Sometimes it precedes action, but more often it follows it. Begin anyway. You have to step out of your comfort zone, and risk your pride, to earn the reward of finding your confidence.

5. The intricacies of what's in it for you. Time teaches us that we keep nothing in this life until we first give it away. This is true of knowledge, forgiveness, service, love, tolerance, acceptance, and so forth. You have to give to receive. Such a simple point, and yet it's so easy to forget that the giving of ourselves, without a price tag, has to come *first*.

6. Being an online-only activist for good causes. Online is fine, but sooner or later you realize that if you truly want to make a difference, you have to walk the talk too. So don't just rant online for a better world.

Love your family. Be a good neighbor. Practice kindness. Build bridges. Embody what you preach.

7. The pressure to make a big difference all at once. When we're young, it seems like faster is better, but in time we witness the power of "slow and steady" to get results. We come to learn that no act of love, kindness, or generosity, no matter how small, is ever wasted. Anything worth achieving takes dedicated daily effort. Over time, you'll look back and marvel at the results you've achieved.

8. The temptation of quick fixes. The older your eyes grow, the more clearly they can see through the smoke and mirrors of every quick fix. Anything worth achieving takes dedicated daily effort. Period! Honestly, I used to believe that making wishes and saying prayers alone changed things, but now I know that wishes and prayers change *us*, and *we* change things. All details aside, when it comes to making a substantial change in your life—building a business, earning a degree, fostering a new relationship, starting a family, becoming more mindful, or any other personal journey that takes time and commitment—one thing you have to ask yourself is, "Am I willing to spend a little time each day like many people won't, so I can spend the better part of my life like many people can't?" Think about that for a moment. We ultimately become what we repeatedly do. The acquisition of knowledge doesn't mean you're growing—growing happens when what you know changes how you live on a daily basis.

9. Having a calendar jam-packed with exciting, elaborate plans. Don't crowd your life with plans. Leave space. Over time you will learn that many great things happen unplanned, and some big regrets happen by not reaching exactly what was planned. So keep your life ordered and your schedule underbooked. Create a foundation with a soft place to land, a wide margin of error, and room to think and breathe every step of the way.

10. Being in constant control of everything. The older we get, the more we realize how little we actually control. Learn to trust the journey, even when you do not fully understand it. Sometimes what you never wanted or expected turns out to be exactly what you need.

11. Blaming others. Have you ever met a happy person who regularly evades responsibility, blames and points fingers, and makes excuses for their unsatisfying life? We haven't either. Happy people accept responsibility for how their lives unfold. They know that their own happiness is a by-product of their own thinking, beliefs, attitudes, character, and behavior.

12. Winning everyone's approval. It's the strength of your conviction that determines your level of personal success in the long run, not the number of people who agree with every little thing you do. Ultimately, you will know that you've made the right decisions and followed the proper path when there is genuine peace in your heart—not someone else's.

13. Saving overly dramatic people from themselves. Honestly, you can't save some people from themselves, so don't get sucked too deeply into their drama. Those who make perpetual chaos of their lives won't appreciate your interfering with the commotion they've created anyway. They want your sympathy, but they don't want to change. And it's not your job to tell them what's right for them.

14. The selfish and disparaging things others say and do. If you take everything personally, you will inevitably be offended for the rest of your life. At some point it becomes clear that the way people treat you is their problem, and how you react is yours. Start taking full advantage of the amazing freedom that comes to you when you detach from other people's antics.

15. Winning arguments. Don't define your intelligence or self-worth by the number of arguments you have won, but by the number of times you have silently told yourself, "This nonsense is just not worth it!"

16. Judging others for their shortcomings. The older we get, the more we realize how important it is to give others the break we hope the world will give us on our own bad days. Truly, you never know what someone has been through in their life, or what they're going through today. Just be kind, generous, and respectful . . . and then be on your way.

17. Society's obsession with outer beauty. As you grow older, what you look like on the outside becomes less and less of an issue, and who you are on the inside becomes the primary point of interest. You eventually realize that beauty has almost nothing to do with looks—it's who you are as a person, how you make others feel about themselves, and, most important, how you feel about yourself.

18. Fancy and expensive physical possessions. Later in life, your personal wish list for "big ticket" physical possessions tends to get smaller and smaller, because the things you really want and need are the little things that can't be bought.

19. All the shallow relationships that just make you feel more popular. It's nice to have acquaintances. Just don't get carried away and spread yourself too thin. Leave plenty of time for those who matter most. Your time is extremely limited, and sooner or later you just want to be around the few people who make you smile for all the right reasons.

20. Distant future possibilities. As time passes, you naturally have more of it behind you and less in front of you. But that doesn't really matter, because the good life always begins right now, when you stop waiting for a better one. Some people wait all day for five p.m., all week for Friday, all year for the holidays, all their lives for happiness. The secret to happiness and peace is letting this moment be what it is, instead of what you think it should be—and then making the very best of it.

Afterthoughts on Making the Best of the Next 20 Years

As you continue to travel the road of life, do your best to avoid letting anyone or anything get in the way of your joy. Live a life that sizzles and pops and makes you laugh out loud every day. Because you don't want to get to the end, or to tomorrow, even, and realize that your life is a collection of meetings and "somedays" and errands and empty promises.

Go ahead and sing out loud in the car with the windows down, and dance in your living room, and stay up late laughing, and paint your walls any color you want, and enjoy some sweet wine and chocolate cake. Yes, and go ahead and sleep in on clean white sheets, and throw parties, and paint, and write poetry, and read books so good they make you lose track of time. And just keep living and making God glad that he gave life to someone who loves and cherishes the gift . . .

Think deeply.

Speak gently.

Love lots.

Laugh often.

Work hard.

Give back.

Expect less.

Be present.

Be kind.

Be honest.

Be true to yourself.

10 WAYS Successful People START Their Mornings

THE DAY MAY have twenty-four hours of equal length, but every hour is not created equal. Beginning the day with a purpose and a plan increases your chances of success. Here are ten smart ways to start your day:

1. Get an early start.

Whether you work from home or commute to an office, the more time you've had to digest the latest news and obstacles ahead, the greater your chances of getting the most out of your day.

2. Clarify and review your priorities.

What is your number one goal right now? What's most important to you? What makes you happy? Design your time around these things. Remember, time is your greatest limited resource, because no matter how hard you try, you can't work 25/8.

3. Prune any nonessential commitments for the day.

The mark of a successful person is the ability to set aside the "somewhat important" things in order to accomplish the vital ones first. When you're crystal clear about your priorities, you can painlessly arrange them in the right order and discard the activities and commitments that do not support the ones at the top of your list.

4. Exercise.

Other than the obvious health benefits, movement increases brain function and decreases stress levels. Developing a consistent habit of exercising is a discipline that will carry over into your business day—Apple CEO Tim Cook is in the gym by five a.m. every morning. If you can, go outside for a walk, or jump on the treadmill and start out slow. This will jump-start your metabolism and your day.

5. Eat a healthly breakfast.

Your brain and body speed are a function of what you take in. Bagels, muffins, and sugars have the tendency to slow you down. Fruits, proteins, and grains help fuel a consistent stream of energy without the sudden drop-off.

6. Kiss your partner good-bye.

It sounds cheesy, but acknowledging your partner (and kids) mentally relaxes you, allowing you to focus on the day ahead. Don't lose sight of the fact that you're striving to be successful so they may benefit as well.

7. Practice fifteen minutes of positive visualization.

Spend a few minutes thinking of everything you're grateful for: in yourself, among your family and friends, in your career. After that, visualize everything you want in your life as if you had it today.

8. Eat that frog.

Brian Tracy's classic time-management book, *Eat That Frog!*, gets its title from a Mark Twain quote that says, if you eat a live frog first thing in the morning, you've got it behind you for the rest of the day, and nothing else will be more difficult. In other words, get the tough stuff done first.

9. Connect with the right people.

Successful people associate with people who are like-minded, focused, and supportive. These people create energy when they enter the room, compared with those who create energy when they leave. Connecting with these positive people in the morning can set you up for a positive day.

10. Stay informed.

Whether you prefer National Public Radio or *The Wall Street Journal*, spend a few minutes each morning learning about what is going on in the world. Not only will it educate you, it may change your perspective or inspire your actions for the day.

12 CHOICES WINNERS
Make Every Day

AT THE END of the day, whether you choose to go with it, flow with it, resist it, change it, or hide from it, life goes on. If what you did today didn't turn out as you'd hoped, tomorrow is a new opportunity to do it differently, or to do nothing at all. What's important is to realize that you have a choice. Here are twelve choices winners make every day:

1. They don't give up on the things they believe in.
If J. K. Rowling had stopped after being turned down by multiple publishers for years, there would be no Harry Potter. If Howard Schultz gave up after being turned down by banks more than two hundred times, there would be no Starbucks. One thing's for sure: if you give up on your dreams too soon, you will miss out on seeing them become a reality.

2. They work with, and spend time with, the right people.
A day spent with the right people is always a day well spent. Sometimes the most ordinary ideas and projects can be made extraordinary simply by discussing them and doing them with the right people.

3. They concentrate on the present.

Today is a new day. Don't let your history interfere with your destiny. It doesn't matter what you did or where you were; what matters is where you are and what you're doing now. Never give up on yourself, and never abandon your values and dreams. As long as you make mistakes, you're still human. And as long as you keep trying, there's still hope.

4. They maintain a positive attitude.

Only you can change your life—no one can do it for you. Happiness always comes from within, and it's found in the present moment by making peace with the past and looking forward to the future. Each morning when you open your eyes, think only three things first: Thank you, thank you, and thank you. Then set out to make the best use of the gift of this day that you can.

5. They endure the pain.

Maybe there's something you're afraid to say, or someone you're afraid to love, or somewhere you're afraid to go. Maybe it's going to hurt. Maybe it's going to hurt because it matters, and because it expands your horizons. Remember, pain isn't always a bad thing; sometimes it's just another step toward personal growth.

6. They ignore the naysayers.

Everyone has unique gifts. People's opinion of you means nothing in the long run, unless that person is *you*.

7. They live through love.

Every human thought, word, or deed is based on fear or love. Fear is the energy that contracts, closes down, draws in, hides, hoards, and harms. Love is the energy that expands, opens up, sends out, reveals, shares, and heals. The only question is: What choice will you make today?

8. They accept 100 percent responsibility for their current situation.

The next five years can be the best five years of your life, or just another five years. The decision is yours. The best part of your life will start on the day you decide your life is your own—no one to lean on, rely on, or blame.

9. They take action and plant the right seeds.

Take positive action and plant the right seeds in your life right now. Be mindful of the seeds you plant, as they will become the crop you harvest in the future.

10. They don't lose themselves in the commotion.

There are two things you shouldn't waste your time on: things that don't matter and people who don't think you matter. Regardless of the situation, don't lose yourself. Stay true to your path, and keep moving forward.

11. They appreciate what they have.

Sometimes people throw away something good for something better only to find out later that good was actually good enough and better never even came close. When you appreciate what you have, what you have appreciates in value. When you truly appreciate your life, you'll find that you have more of it to live.

12. They make a positive difference.

Being the richest man or woman in the cemetery doesn't matter; going to bed every night knowing that you're making a positive difference in the world is what matters.

12 THINGS HIGHLY Productive People Do Differently

BEING HIGHLY PRODUCTIVE is not an innate talent, it's simply a matter of organizing your life so that you can efficiently get the right things done. What can you do to increase your own productivity? Here are some ideas to get you started:

1. Create and observe a "to-don't" list.

A "to-don't" list is a list of things *not* to do. It might seem amusing, but it's an incredibly useful tool for keeping track of unproductive habits, like checking Facebook and Twitter, randomly browsing news websites, and so on. Create your "to don't" list and post it in your workspace where you can see it.

2. Organize your space and data.

Highly productive people have systems in place to help them find what they need when they need it—they can quickly locate the information required to support their activities. When you're disorganized, that extra time spent looking for a phone number, an e-mail address, or a certain file forces you to drop your focus. Keeping both your living and working spaces organized is crucial.

3. Ruthlessly eliminate distractions while you work.

Eliminating all distractions for a set time while you work is one of the most effective ways to get things done. So lock your door, put up a sign, turn off your phone, close your e-mail application, and disconnect your Internet connection. You can't remain in hiding forever, but you can be twice as productive while you are. Do whatever it takes to create a quiet, distraction-free environment where you can focus on your work.

4. Set and pursue S.M.A.R.T. goals.

These goals must be Specific, Measurable, Attainable, Relevant, and Timely.

5. Break down goals into realistic, high-impact tasks.

Take your primary goal and divide it into smaller and smaller chunks until you have a list of realistic tasks, each of which can be accomplished in a few hours or less. Then work on the next unfinished, available task that will have the greatest impact at the current time. And each of these smaller goals is supported by even more granular subgoals and daily tasks. It is these small daily tasks that, over time, drive larger achievement.

6. *Work when your mind is fresh, and put first things first.*

Highly productive people recognize that not all hours are created equal, and they strategically account for this when planning their day. For most of us, our minds operate at peak performance in the morning hours when we're well rested. So obviously it would be foolish to use this time for a trivial task like reading e-mails. These peak performance hours should be 100 percent dedicated to working on the tasks that bring you closer to your goals.

7. Focus on being productive, not being busy.

Don't just get things done—get the *right* things done. Results are always more important than the time it takes to achieve them. Stop and ask yourself if what you're working on is worth the effort. Is it bringing you in the same direction as your goals? Don't get caught up in odd jobs, even those that seem urgent, unless they are also important.

8. Commit your undivided attention to one thing at a time.

Stop multitasking, and start getting the important things done properly. Single-tasking helps you focus more intently on one task so you can finish it properly, rather than having many tasks started and nothing finished. Quickly switching from task to task makes the mind less efficient.

9. Work in ninety-minute intervals.

In his *New York Times* bestseller *The Way We're Working Isn't Working*, Tony Schwartz makes the case for working no more than ninety consecutive minutes before a short break. Do it for the sake of your mind, body, and productivity.

10. Reply to e-mails, voicemails, and texts at a set time.

This ties into the ideas of single-tasking and distraction avoidance. Set specific time slots two or three times a day to deal with incoming communication, and set a reasonable maximum duration for each time slot. Unless an emergency arises, be militant about sticking to this practice.

11. Invest a little time to save a lot of time.

Think about the tasks you perform over and over throughout a workweek. Is there a more efficient way? Is there a shortcut you can learn? Is there a way to automate or delegate them? Perhaps you can complete a particular task in twenty minutes, and it would take two hours to put in place a more efficient method. Bottom line: The more you automate and delegate, the more you can get done with the same level of effort.

12. Narrow the number of ventures you're involved in.

In other words, say no when you should. Working simultaneously on too many fronts at once causes all activities to slow down, stand still, and sometimes even slide backward. Focus on what matters most, and say no more.

PRODUCTIVITY QUESTIONS TO MAKE YOU THINK

What could you AVOID to *improve* your productivity?

What is WORSE, *failing* or *never trying*?

When it's all SAID and DONE, will you have *said* *more* than you've *done*?

If not NOW, then *when*?

So far, what has been the primary FOCUS of your recent *life*?

What do you DO when you feel like *giving up*?

What are you one step CLOSER to *today* than you were yesterday?

What PEOPLE and ACTIVITIES *energize* you?

What are you GLAD you *quit*?

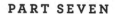

PART SEVEN

Goals and Success

*In the end, you're going to succeed because
you're crazy enough to think you can.*

HOW TO WALK ON WATER

RECENTLY I WAS relaxing at the water's edge of a local beach when a young boy ran full speed right by me and into the shallow surf. He continuously hopped up and down as he was running forward, kicking his little legs in the air and across the surface of the water before inevitably falling face-first into the waves. He got back up and repeated this act several times, each time with more determination than the previous attempt. It became obvious that he was trying to run across the surface of the water. I couldn't help but laugh. His combined levels of determination and exertion were priceless.

After several attempts, he noticed my laughter and walked over to me. "What's so funny?" he asked.

"You remind me of me, and it makes me smile," I said.

"Do you know how to walk on water?" he asked. "Like a superhero?"

"Well, I think I can help you out," I said. "Let me give you a few pointers."

Curious, the boy sat down on the sand next to me. His mother scurried over, worried . . . but I reassured her that her son wasn't bothering me. Relieved, perhaps, to have her son sitting safely on the sand instead of flying face-first through the air, she went back to her beach chair twenty feet away and continued a conversation with another lady.

"So, you want to walk on water, eh?" I asked. He nodded his head anxiously.

A Rough Summary of What I Told Him

1. Make sure you were born to walk on water. You must follow your heart, and be who you were born to be. Some of us were born to be musicians . . . to communicate intricate thoughts and rousing feelings with the strings of a guitar. Some of us were born to be poets . . . to touch people's hearts with exquisite words. Some of us were born to be entrepreneurs . . . to create growth and opportunity where others saw rubbish. And still some of us were born to walk on water . . . to invent the capability of doing so. If you're going to walk on water, you'd better feel it in every fiber of your being. You'd better be born to do it!

2. Decide that nothing can stop you. Being born to walk on water isn't enough by itself. We must each decide to accept our calling. Unfortunately, most of us make excuses instead. "But I might drown trying," we say. Or, "But I have a family to think about first." Walking on water, or doing anything that hasn't been done before, requires absolute, unconditional dedication. The only person who can control your level of dedication is you. If you're serious about walking on water, you must decide that nothing—not gravity, not a group of naysayers, *nothing*—can stop you!

3. Work on it for real. While many of us decide at some point during the course of our lives that we want to answer our calling—to accomplish our own version of walking on water—only an astute few of us actually work on it. By "working on it," I mean truly devoting oneself to the end result. The rest of us never act on our decision. Or at best, we pretend to act on it by putting forth an uninspired, half-ass effort. But to truly walk on water, you'll have to study physics, rheology, hydrophobic substances, and so on . . . and then you'll have to define and redefine next-generation theories and complex hypotheses, which must be tested relentlessly. When the tests fail, you must be ready to edit your theories and test them again. This kind of work, the real kind, is precisely what enables us to make the impossible possible.

4. Let the whole world know what you're up to. When you're trying to walk on water, or do anything that nobody else has done before, life can get lonely pretty quickly. To keep your motivation thriving, it's important to let others know that you're attempting to defeat the formerly impossible. Don't be shy! Let the whole world know that you're trying to walk on water. No doubt, it'll place a bit of extra pressure on your back, and you'll almost certainly hear some laughter in the crowd. But this kind of pressure fuels motivation, which is exactly what you'll need to accomplish such a colossal undertaking. And when you finally do succeed, the last bit of laughter heard will be your own.

5. Value the people who value your ambitions. When most people hear about your "mission impossible" aspirations, their natural reaction may be to roll their eyes, call you crazy, and tell you to quit being foolish. But fortunately, the world is also inhabited by pioneers and believers who see the value in your dreams. These people understand that achieving the formerly impossible is one of the greatest gifts human beings possess. They'll likely give you tips, bits of assistance, and the extra push you need to succeed. These are extraordinary people, and you'll want to surround yourself with them because they will ultimately assist you over the hurdles and across the surface of the water. Think of them as an influential personal-support team. Without them, walking on water will be a far more difficult feat, if not completely impossible.

6. Ignore the naysayers. No matter how much progress you make, there will always be the people who insist that walking on water is impossible, simply because it hasn't been done before. Or they may incessantly suggest that the idea as a whole is utterly ridiculous because nobody really cares about walking on water anyway. When you come across these people, don't try to reason with them. Instead, forget that they exist. They will only waste your time and energy.

7. Prepare yourself for the pain. Even though you're no longer mindlessly running face-first into the oncoming ocean surf, but instead forming complex theories based on the studies of rheology and fluid viscosity, it doesn't mean you won't experience your fair share of pain. You're in the business of walking on water, of doing something that has never been done before. You'll likely get a waterlogged lung on a regular basis. But the pain will seem like a small price to pay when you become the first person to jog across the rapids of the Mississippi River.

8. Enjoy the pain of your greatest challenge. Superheroes aren't real. In real life nobody has ever walked on water. But lots of people have achieved formerly impossible feats, and continue to enjoy the possibilities of new challenges. These people will all tell you there's nothing more gratifying than the thrill of your greatest challenge. The inherent pains along the way are simply mile markers on your trip to the finish line. When you finally do finish, you may actually find yourself missing the daily grind. Ultimately, you'll realize that pleasure and pain can be one and the same.

9. Never give up. Never quit. The reason no one has walked on water isn't because people haven't tried. Remember, you just tried several times in a row, and I'm sure many others have too. The reason nobody has succeeded is, simply, that within the scope of modern science and physics, it's currently impossible. But this doesn't mean that with your help it won't become possible in the future. If you were born to do it and truly dedicate yourself to the end result, anything, including walking on water, is entirely possible.

Just a Chance

When we were done talking, the young boy got up and ran back over to his mother. He pointed over to me and I smiled and waved back. Then he said to her, "Mommy, Mommy! That guy just taught me how to walk on water!"

A few moments later she walked over to scold me for supposedly giving out reckless advice. She told me I was giving her son a false sense of hope. I told her all I was giving him was a chance.

12 THINGS SUCCESSFUL People Do Differently

WE'VE ALWAYS BEEN fascinated by people who are consistently successful at what they do—especially those who experience repeated success in many areas of their life throughout their lifetime. In entertainment, we think of Clint Eastwood and Oprah Winfrey. In business, we think of Steve Jobs and Warren Buffett. We all have our own examples of supersuccessful people like these whom we admire. But how do they do it?

Over the years we've studied the lives of numerous successful people. We've read their books, watched their interviews, researched them online, and so forth. And we've learned that most of them were not born into success, but they simply did, and continue to do, things that help them realize their full potential. Here are twelve things they do differently that the rest of us can easily emulate:

1. They create and pursue S.M.A.R.T. goals.

Successful people are objective. They have realistic targets in mind. They know what they are looking for and why they are fighting for it. Successful people create and pursue S.M.A.R.T. goals.

S.M.A.R.T. goals are Specific, Measurable, Attainable, Relevant, and Timely. When you identify S.M.A.R.T. goals that are truly important to you, you become motivated to figure out ways to attain them. You develop the necessary attitude, abilities, and skills. You can achieve almost any goal you set if you plan your steps wisely and establish a time frame that allows you to carry out those steps. Goals that once seemed far away and out of reach eventually move closer and become attainable, not because your goals shrink, but because you grow and expand to match them.

2. They take decisive and immediate action.

Sadly, very few people ever live to become the success story they dream about. And there's one simple reason why: They never take action!

The acquisition of knowledge doesn't mean you're growing. Growing happens when what you know changes how you live. So many people live in a complete daze. Actually, they don't "live." They simply "get by" because they never take the necessary action to make things happen—to seek their dreams.

It doesn't matter if you have a genius IQ and a PhD in quantum physics, you can't change anything or make any sort of real-world progress without taking action. There's a huge difference between knowing how to do something and actually doing it. Knowledge and intelligence are both useless without action. It's as simple as that.

Success hinges on the simple act of making a decision to live—to absorb yourself in the process of going after your dreams and goals. So make that decision. And take action.

3. They focus on being productive, not being busy.

Take a quick look around. The busy outnumber the productive by a wide margin.

Busy people are rushing all over the place, and running late half of the time. They're heading to work, conferences, meetings, social engagements. They barely have enough free time for family get-togethers and they rarely get enough sleep. Yet business e-mails are shooting out of their smartphones like BB-gun pellets, and their daily planner is jammed to the brim with obligations.

Their busy schedule gives them an elevated sense of importance. But it's all an illusion. They're like hamsters running on a wheel.

The solution: Slow down. Breathe. Review your commitments and goals. Put first things first. Do one thing at a time. Start now. Take a short break in two hours. Repeat.

And always remember, results are more important than the time it takes to achieve them.

4. They make logical, informed decisions.

Sometimes we do things that are permanently foolish simply because we are temporarily upset or excited.

Although emotional "gut instincts" are effective in certain fleeting situations, when it comes to generating long-term, sustained growth in any area of life, emotional decisions often lead a person astray.

5. They avoid the trap of trying to make things perfect.

Many of us are perfectionists in our own right. We set high bars for ourselves and put our best foot forward. We dedicate copious amounts of time and attention to our work to maintain our high personal standards. Our passion for excellence drives us to run the extra mile, never stopping, never relenting. And this dedication toward perfection undoubtedly helps us achieve results . . . so long as we don't get carried away.

But what happens when we do get carried away with perfectionism?

We become disgruntled and discouraged when we fail to meet the (impossibly high) standards we set for ourselves, making us reluctant to take on new challenges or even finish tasks we've already started.

Our insistence on dotting every *i* and crossing every *t* breeds inefficiency, causing major delays, stress overload, and subpar results.

True perfectionists have a hard time starting things and an even harder time finishing them, always. I have a friend who has wanted to start a graphic design business for several years. But she hasn't yet. Why? When you sift through her extensive list of excuses, it comes down to one simple problem: She is a perfectionist. Which means she doesn't, and never will, think she's good enough at graphic design to own and operate her own graphic design business.

Remember, the real world doesn't reward perfectionists. It rewards people who get things done. And the only way to get things done is to be imperfect 99 percent of the time. Only by wading through years of practice and imperfection can we begin to achieve momentary glimpses of perfection. So make a decision. Take action, learn from the outcome, and repeat this method over and over again in all walks of life.

6. They work outside of their comfort zone.

The number one thing we persistently see holding smart people back is their own reluctance to accept an opportunity simply because they don't think they're ready. In other words, they feel uncomfortable and believe they require additional knowledge, skill, and experience before they can aptly partake in the opportunity. Sadly, this is the kind of thinking that stifles personal growth and success.

The truth is nobody ever feels 100 percent ready when an opportunity arises—because most great opportunities in life force us to grow emotionally and intellectually. They force us to stretch ourselves and our comfort zones, which means we won't feel totally comfortable at first. And when we don't feel comfortable, we don't feel ready.

Significant moments of opportunity for personal growth and success will come and go throughout your lifetime. If you are looking to make positive changes and new breakthroughs in your life, you will need to embrace these moments of opportunity even though you will never feel 100 percent ready for them.

7. They keep things simple.

"Simplicity is the ultimate sophistication" is a quote we've always loved. And nothing could be closer to the truth. Here in the twenty-first century, where information moves at the speed of light and opportunities for innovation seem endless, we have an abundant array of choices when it comes to designing our lives and careers. But sadly, an abundance of choice often leads to complication, confusion, and inaction.

Several business and marketing studies have shown that the more product choices a consumer is faced with, the fewer products they typically buy. After all, narrowing down the best product from a pool of three choices is certainly a lot easier than narrowing down the best product from a pool of three hundred choices. If the purchasing decision is tough to make, most people will just give up. Likewise, if you complicate your life by inundating yourself with too many choices, your subconscious mind will give up.

The solution is to simplify. If you're selling a product line, keep it simple. And if you're trying to make a decision about something in your life, don't waste all your time evaluating every last detail of every possible option. Choose something that you think will work and give it a shot. If it doesn't work out, learn what you can from the experience, choose something else, and keep pressing forward.

8. They focus on making small, continuous improvements.

Henry Ford once said, "Nothing is particularly hard if you divide it into small pieces." The same concept can be configured as a question: How do you eat an elephant? Answer: One bite at a time. This philosophy holds true for achieving your biggest goals. Making small, positive changes—eating a little more healthfully, exercising a little longer, creating some small productive habits, for example—is an amazing way to get excited about life and slowly reach the level of success you aspire to.

Start with just one activity and make a plan for how you will deal with troubles when they arise. For instance, let's revisit an example we used earlier in this book: if you're trying to lose weight, come up with a list of healthful snacks you can eat when you get the craving for snacks. It will be hard in the beginning, but it will get easier. And that's the whole point. As your strength grows, you can take on bigger challenges.

9. They measure and track their progress.

Successful people are not only working in their job/business, they are also working on it. They step back and assess their progress regularly. They track themselves against their goals and clearly know what needs to be done in order for them to excel and accelerate.

You can't control what you don't properly measure. If you track the wrong things, you'll be completely blind to potential opportunities as they appear over the horizon. Imagine if, while running a small business, you made it a point to keep track of how many pencils and paper clips you used. Would that make any sense? No! Because pencils and paper clips are not a measure of what's important for a business. Pencils and paper clips have no bearing on income, customer satisfaction, market growth, and the like.

The proper approach is to figure out what your number one goal is and then track the things that directly relate to achieving that goal. We recommend that you take some time right now to identify your number one goal, identify the most important things for you to keep track of, and then begin tracking them immediately. On a weekly basis, plug the numbers into a spreadsheet and use the data to create weekly or monthly trend graphs so you can visualize your progress. Then fine-tune your actions to get those trends to grow in your favor.

10. They maintain a positive outlook as they learn from their mistakes.

Successful people concentrate on the positives—they look for the silver lining in every situation. They know that it is their positivity that will take them to greatness. If you want to be successful, you need to have a positive outlook on life. Life will test you again and again. If you give in to internal negativity, you will never be able to achieve the marks you have targeted.

Remember, every mistake you make is progress. Mistakes teach you important lessons. Every time you make one, you're one step closer to your goal. The only mistake that can truly hurt you is choosing to do nothing simply because you're too scared to make a mistake.

So don't hesitate—don't doubt yourself! Don't let your own negativity sabotage you. Learn what you can and press forward.

11. They spend time with the right people.

You are the sum of the people you spend the most time with. If you hang with the wrong people, they will negatively affect you. But if you hang with the right people, you will become far more capable and successful than you ever could have been alone. Find your tribe and work together to make a difference in all of your lives.

12. They maintain balance in life.

If you ask most people to summarize what they want out of life, they'll shout out a list of things like: "fall in love," "make money," "spend time with family," "find happiness," "achieve goals"—the list goes on. But sadly, a lot of people don't balance their life properly to achieve these things. Typically they'll achieve one or two of them while completely neglecting the rest.

While drive and focus are important, if you're going to get things done right, and be truly successful, you need to balance the various dimensions of your life. Completely neglecting one dimension for another only leads to long-term frustration and stress.

30 THINGS to STOP
Doing to Yourself

AS THE AUTHOR Maria Robinson once said, "Nobody can go back and start a new beginning, but anyone can start today and make a new ending." But before you can begin this process of transformation, you have to stop doing the things that have been holding you back. Here are some ideas to get you started:

1. Stop spending time with the wrong people.

Life is too short to spend time with people who suck the happiness out of you. If someone wants you in their life, they'll make room for you. You shouldn't have to fight for a spot. Never, ever beg for the attention of someone who continuously overlooks your worth. And remember, it's not the people who stand by your side when you're at your best, but the ones who stand beside you when you're at your worst who are your true friends.

2. Stop running from your problems.

Face them head-on. No, it won't be easy. We aren't supposed to be able to instantly solve problems. In fact, we're made to get upset, sad, hurt, stumble, and fall. Because that's the whole purpose of living—to face problems, learn, adapt, and solve them over the course of time. This is what ultimately molds us into the person we become.

3. Stop lying to yourself.
Our lives improve only when we take chances, and the first and most difficult chance we can take is to be honest with ourselves.

4. Stop putting your own needs on the back burner.
The most painful thing is losing yourself in the process of loving someone too much, and forgetting that you are special too. Yes, help others; but help yourself too. If there was ever a moment to follow your passion and do something that matters to you, that moment is now.

5. Stop trying to be someone you're not.
One of the greatest challenges in life is being yourself in a world that's trying to make you like everyone else. Someone will always be prettier, someone will always be smarter, someone will always be younger, but they will never be you. Don't change so people will like you. Be yourself and the right people will love the real you.

6. Stop trying to hold on to the past.
You can't start the next chapter of your life if you keep rereading your last one.

7. Stop being scared to make a mistake.
Doing something and getting it wrong is at least ten times more productive than doing nothing. Every success has a trail of failures behind it, and every failure is leading toward success. You end up regretting the things you did *not* do far more than the things you did.

8. Stop berating yourself for old mistakes.

We all make mistakes, have struggles, and even regret things in our past. But you are not your mistakes, you are not your struggles, and you are here *now* with the power to shape your day and your future. Every single thing that has ever happened in your life is preparing you for a moment that is yet to come.

9. Stop trying to buy happiness.

Many of the things we desire are expensive. But the truth is, the things that really satisfy us are totally free—love, laughter, and working on our passions.

10. Stop looking to others for happiness.

If you're not happy with who you are on the inside, you won't be happy in a long-term relationship with anyone else either. You have to create stability in your own life first before you can share it with someone else.

11. Stop waiting.

Don't think too much or you'll create a problem that wasn't even there in the first place. Evaluate situations and take decisive action. You cannot change what you refuse to confront. Making progress involves risk. Period! You can't make it to second base with your foot on first.

12. Stop thinking you're not ready.

Nobody ever feels 100 percent ready when an opportunity arises. Most great opportunities in life force us to grow beyond our comfort zones, which means we won't feel totally comfortable at first.

13. Stop getting involved in relationships for the wrong reasons.

Relationships must be chosen wisely. It's better to be alone than to be in bad company. There's no need to rush. If something is meant to be, it will happen—in the right time, with the right person, and for the best reason. Fall in love when you're ready, not when you're lonely.

14. Stop rejecting new relationships just because old ones didn't work.

In life you'll realize that there is a purpose for everyone you meet. Some will test you, some will use you, and some will teach you. But most important, some will bring out the best in you.

15. Stop trying to compete against everyone else.

Don't worry about what others are doing better than you. Concentrate on beating your own records every day. Success is a battle between *you* and *yourself* only.

16. Stop being jealous of others.

Jealousy is the art of counting someone else's blessings instead of your own. Ask yourself this: "What's something I have that everyone wants?"

17. Stop complaining and feeling sorry for yourself.

You may not see or understand everything the moment it happens, and it may be tough. But reflect back on those negative curveballs thrown at you in the past. You'll often see that eventually they led you to a better place, person, state of mind, or situation.

18. Stop holding grudges.

Don't live your life with hate in your heart. Forgiveness is the answer . . . let go, find peace, liberate yourself! And remember, forgiveness is not just for other people, it's for you too. If you must forgive yourself, move on, and try to do better next time.

19. Stop letting others bring you down to their level.

Refuse to lower your standards to accommodate those who refuse to raise theirs.

20. Stop wasting time explaining yourself to others.

Your friends don't need it and your enemies won't believe it anyway. Just do what you know in your heart is right.

21. Stop doing the same things over and over without taking a break.

The time to take a deep breath is when you don't have time for it. If you keep doing what you're doing, you'll keep getting what you're getting. Sometimes you need to distance yourself to see things clearly.

22. Stop overlooking the beauty of small moments.

Enjoy the little things, because one day you may look back and discover they were the big things. The best portion of your life will be the small, nameless moments you spend smiling with someone who matters to you.

23. Stop trying to make things perfect.

Making mistakes is always better than faking perfection. Live your life accepting that you're not perfect, rather than spending your whole life pretending to be.

24. Stop following the path of least resistance.

Life is not easy, especially when you plan on achieving something worthwhile. Don't take the easy way out. Do something extraordinary.

25. Stop acting like everything is fine if it isn't.

It's OK to fall apart for a little while. You don't always have to pretend to be strong, and there is no need to constantly prove that everything is going well. You shouldn't be concerned with what other people are thinking, either—cry if you need to, it's healthy to shed your tears. The sooner you do, the sooner you will be able to smile again.

26. Stop blaming others for your troubles.

The extent to which you can achieve your dreams depends on the extent to which you take responsibility for your life. When you blame others for what you're going through, you deny responsibility—you give others power over that part of your life.

27. Stop trying to be everything to everyone.

Doing so is impossible, and trying will only burn you out. But making one person smile *can* change the world. Maybe not the whole world, but their world. So narrow your focus.

28. Stop worrying so much.

Worry will not strip tomorrow of its burdens, it will strip today of its joy. One way to check if something is worth mulling over is to ask yourself this question: "Will this matter in one year's time? Three years? Five years?" If not, then it's not worth worrying about.

29. Stop focusing on what you don't want to happen.

Focus on what you *do* want to happen. Positive thinking is at the forefront of every great success story. If you awake every morning with the thought that something wonderful will happen in your life today, and you pay close attention, you'll often find that you're right.

30. Stop being ungrateful.

No matter how good or bad you have it, wake up each day thankful for your life. Someone somewhere else is desperately fighting for theirs. Instead of thinking about what you're missing, try thinking about what you have that everyone else is missing.

30 THINGS to START Doing for Yourself

OUR PREVIOUS SECTION, "30 Things to Stop Doing to Yourself," was well received by most of our readers when we published it on our blog, but several of you suggested that we follow it up with a list of things to *start doing*. In one reader's words: "I would love to see you revisit each of these thirty principles, but instead of presenting us with a 'to-don't' list, present us with a 'to-do' list that we all can start working on today, together." Some folks actually took it one step further and e-mailed us their own revised "to-do" versions of the list.

So we sat down with our original article and the two readers' revisions as a guide, and a couple hours later finalized a new list of thirty things, which ended up being, we think, a perfect complement to the original.

Here it is, a positive "to-do" list for the upcoming year—thirty things to start doing for yourself:

1. Start spending time with the right people.

These are the people you enjoy, who love and appreciate you, and who encourage you to improve in healthy and exciting ways. They are the ones who make you feel more alive, and not only embrace who you are now, but also unconditionally embrace and embody who you want to be.

2. Start facing your problems head-on.

It isn't your problems that define you, but how you react to them and recover from them. Problems will not disappear unless you take action. Do what you can, when you can, and acknowledge what you've done. It's all about taking baby steps in the right direction, inch by inch. These inches count; they add up to yards and miles in the long run.

3. Start being honest with yourself about everything.

Be honest about what's right, as well as what needs to be changed. Be honest about what you want to achieve and who you want to become. Search your soul for the truth so that you truly know who you are. Once you do, you'll have a better understanding of where you are now and how you got here, and you'll be better equipped to identify where you want to go and how to get there.

4. Start making your own happiness a priority.

Your needs matter. If you don't value yourself, look out for yourself, and stick up for yourself, you're sabotaging yourself. Remember, it *is* possible to take care of your own needs while simultaneously caring for those around you. And once your needs are met, you will likely be far more capable of helping those who need you most.

5. Start being yourself, genuinely and proudly.

Trying to be anyone else is a waste of the person you are. Be yourself. Embrace that individual inside you who has ideas, strengths, and beauty like no one else. Be the person you know yourself to be—the best version of you—on your terms. Above all, be true to *you*, and if you cannot put your heart in it, take yourself out of it.

6. Start noticing and living in the present.

Right now is a miracle. Right now is the only moment guaranteed to you. Right now is life. So stop thinking about how great things will be in the future. Stop dwelling on what did or didn't happen in the past. Learn to be in the "here and now" and experience life as it's happening. Appreciate the world for the beauty that it holds, right now.

7. Start valuing the lessons your mistakes teach you.

Mistakes are OK; they're the stepping-stones of progress. If you're not failing from time to time, you're not trying hard enough and you're not learning. Take risks, stumble, fall, and then get up and try again. Appreciate that you are pushing yourself, learning, growing, and improving. Significant achievements are almost invariably realized at the end of a long road of failures. One of the "mistakes" you fear might just be the link to your greatest achievement yet.

8. Start being more polite to yourself.

Let's revisit a question we asked earlier in this book: If you had a friend who spoke to you in the same way that you sometimes speak to yourself, how long would you allow that person to be your friend? Remember, the way you treat yourself sets the standard for others. You must respect who you are or no one else will.

9. Start enjoying the things you already have.

Too many of us think we'll be happy when we reach a certain level in life—a level we see others operating at—your boss with her corner office, that friend of a friend who owns a mansion on the beach. Unfortunately, it takes a while before you get there, and when you get there you'll likely have a new destination in mind. You'll end up spending your whole life working toward something new without ever stopping to enjoy the things you have now. So take a quiet moment every morning when you first awake to appreciate where you are and what you already have.

10. Start creating your own happiness.

If you are waiting for someone else to make you happy, you're missing out. Smile because you can. Choose happiness. Be the change you want to see in the world. Be happy with who you are now, and let your positivity inspire your journey into tomorrow. Happiness is often found when and where you decide to seek it. If you look for happiness within the opportunities you have, you will eventually find it. But if you constantly look for something else, unfortunately, you'll find that too.

11. Start giving your ideas and dreams a chance.

In life, it's rarely about getting a chance, it's about taking a chance. You'll never be 100 percent sure it will work, but you can always be 100 percent sure doing nothing won't work. Most of the time you just have to go for it! And no matter how it turns out, it always ends up just the way it should be. Either you succeed or you learn something.

12. Start believing that you're ready for the next step.

You are ready! Think about it. You have everything you need right now to take the next small, realistic step forward. So embrace the opportunities that come your way, and accept the challenges—they're gifts that will help you to grow.

13. Start entering new relationships for the right reasons.

Enter new relationships with dependable, honest people who reflect the person you are and the person you want to be. Choose friends you are proud to know, people you admire, who show you love and respect—people who reciprocate your kindness and commitment.

14. Start giving new people you meet a chance.

Appreciate the possibility of new relationships as you naturally let go of old ones that no longer work. Trust your judgment. Embrace new relationships, knowing that you are entering into unfamiliar territory. Be ready to learn, be ready for a challenge, and be ready to meet someone who might just change your life forever.

15. Start competing against an earlier version of yourself.

Be inspired by others, appreciate others, learn from others, but know that competing against them is a waste of time. You are in competition with one person and one person only—yourself. You are competing to be the best you can be. Aim to break your own personal records.

16. Start cheering for other people's victories.

Start noticing what you like about others and tell them. Having an appreciation for how amazing the people around you are leads to good places—productive, fulfilling, peaceful places. So be happy for those who are making progress. Cheer for their victories, and sooner or later, they'll start cheering for you.

17. Start looking for the silver lining in tough situations.

When things are hard and you feel down, take a few deep breaths and look for the silver lining—the small glimmers of hope. Remind yourself that you can and will grow stronger from these hard times. And remain conscious of your blessings and victories—all the things in your life that are right. Focus on what you have, not on what you haven't.

18. Start forgiving yourself and others.

We've all been hurt by our own decisions and by others. And while the pain of these experiences is normal, sometimes it lingers for too long. We relive the pain over and over and have a hard time letting go. So forgive yourself for the bad decisions you made, for the times you lacked understanding, for the choices that hurt others and yourself. Forgive others for being young and reckless too. These are all vital lessons. And what matters most right now is your willingness to learn and grow from them.

19. Start helping those around you.

Care about people. Guide them if you know a better way. The more you help others, the more they will want to help you. Love and kindness begets love and kindness.

20. Start listening to your own inner voice.

If it helps, discuss your ideas with those closest to you, but give yourself enough room to follow your own intuition. Be true to yourself. Say what you need to say. Do what you know in your heart is right.

21. Start being attentive to your stress level and take short breaks.

Slow down. Breathe. Give yourself permission to pause, regroup, and move forward with clarity and purpose. When you're at your busiest, a brief recess can rejuvenate your mind and increase your productivity. These short breaks will help you regain your sanity and reflect on your recent actions so you can be sure they're in line with your goals.

22. Start noticing the beauty of small moments.

Instead of waiting for the big things to happen—marriage, kids, big promotion, winning the lottery—find happiness in the small things that happen every day. Little things like having a quiet cup of coffee in the early morning, or the delicious taste and smell of a homemade meal, or the pleasure of sharing something you enjoy with someone else, or holding hands with your partner. Noticing these small pleasures on a daily basis makes a big difference in the quality of your life.

23. Start accepting things when they are less than perfect.

One of the biggest challenges for people who want to improve themselves and improve the world is learning to accept things as they are. Sometimes it's better to accept and appreciate the world as it is, and people as they are, rather than trying to make everything and everyone conform to an impossible ideal. No, you shouldn't accept a life of mediocrity, but learn to love and value things when they are less than perfect.

24. Start working toward your goals every single day.

Remember, the journey of a thousand miles begins with one step. Whatever it is you dream about, start taking small, logical steps every day to make it happen. Get out there and *do* something! The harder you work, the luckier you will become. While many of us decide at some point during the course of our lives that we want to answer our calling, only an astute few of us actually work on it. By "working on it," I mean consistently devoting oneself to the end result.

25. Start being more open about how you feel.

If you're hurting, give yourself the necessary space and time to hurt, but be open about it. Talk to those closest to you. Tell them the truth about how you feel. Let them listen. The simple act of getting things off your chest and into the open is your first step toward feeling good again.

26. Start taking full accountability for your own life.

Own your choices and mistakes and be willing to take the necessary steps to improve upon them. Either you take accountability for your life or someone else will. And when they do, you'll become a slave to their ideas and dreams instead of a pioneer of your own.

27. Start actively nurturing your most important relationships.

Bring real, honest joy into your life and the lives of those you love simply by telling them how much they mean to you on a regular basis. You can't be everything to everyone, but you can be everything to a few people. Decide who these people are in your life and treat them like royalty. Remember, you don't need a certain number of friends, just a number of friends you can be certain of.

28. Start concentrating on the things you can control.

You can't change everything, but you can always change something. Wasting your time, talent, and emotional energy on things that are beyond your control is a recipe for frustration, misery, and stagnation. Invest your energy in the things you can control, and act on them now.

29. Start focusing on the possibility of positive outcomes.

The mind must believe it *can* do something before it is capable of actually doing it. The way to overcome negative thoughts and destructive emotions is to develop opposing, positive emotions that are stronger and more powerful. Listen to your self-talk and replace negative thoughts with positive ones. Regardless of how a situation seems, focus on what you *do want* to happen, and then take the next positive step forward. No, you can't control everything that happens to you, but you can control how you react to things. Everyone's life has positive and negative aspects—whether you're happy and successful in the long run depends greatly on which aspects you focus on.

30. Start noticing how wealthy you are right now.

Wealth, in a sense, is the ability to fully experience life. Even when times are tough, it's always important to keep things in perspective. You didn't go to sleep hungry last night. You didn't go to sleep outside. You had a choice of what clothes to wear this morning. Some might say you are incredibly wealthy, so remember to be grateful for all the things you *do* have.

HOW TO MAKE
ALL THE DIFFERENCE
IN THE WORLD

EVERY SUNDAY MORNING I take a light jog around a park near my home. There's a lake located in one corner of the park. Each time I jog by this lake, I see the same elderly woman sitting at the water's edge with a small metal cage sitting beside her.

One Sunday my curiosity got the best of me, so I stopped jogging and walked over to her. As I got closer, I realized that the metal cage was in fact a small trap. There were three turtles, unharmed, slowly walking around the base of the trap. She had a fourth turtle in her lap that she was carefully scrubbing with a spongy brush.

"Hello," I said. "I see you here every Sunday morning. If you don't mind my nosiness, I'd love to know what you're doing with these turtles."

She smiled. "I'm cleaning off their shells," she replied. "Anything on a turtle's shell, like algae or scum, reduces the turtle's ability to absorb heat and impedes its ability to swim. It can also corrode and weaken the shell over time."

"Wow! That's really nice of you!" I exclaimed.

She went on: "I spend a couple of hours each Sunday morning relaxing by this lake and helping these little guys out. It's my own strange way of making a difference."

"But don't most freshwater turtles live their whole lives with algae and scum hanging from their shells?" I asked.

"Yep, sadly, they do," she replied.

I scratched my head. "Well, then, don't you think your time could be better spent? I mean, I think your efforts are kind and all, but there are freshwater turtles living in lakes all around the world, and ninety-nine percent of these turtles don't have kind people like you to help them clean off their shells. So, no offense . . . but how exactly are your localized efforts here truly making a difference?"

The woman giggled. She then looked down at the turtle in her lap, scrubbed off the last piece of algae from its shell, and said, "Sweetie, if this little guy could talk, he'd tell you I just made all the difference in the world."

30 CHALLENGES
for 30 Days of Growth

SCIENTISTS HAVE SUGGESTED that, with a little willpower, it takes roughly thirty days for a person to form a new habit. As with mastering anything new, the act of starting and getting beyond the preliminary stage where everything feels awkward is 80 percent of the battle. This is precisely why it's important to make small, positive changes every day over the course of at least a thirty-day period.

And when you start small, you won't need a lot of motivation, either. The simple act of getting started and doing something will give you the momentum you need, and soon you'll find yourself in an upward spiral of changes—one building on the other. When I started doing this in my life, I was so excited about it that I started a blog to share it with the world.

Below you will find thirty challenges to be accomplished over the course of thirty days. If carried out diligently, each of them has the potential to create a new positive habit in your life. Yes, there is some slight overlap between a few of them. And no, you don't have to attempt them all at once. Pick two to five and commit the next thirty days, wholeheartedly, to successfully completing the challenge. Then, once you feel comfortable with these habits, challenge yourself with a few more the following month.

1. Use words that encourage happiness.

Typically, when I ask someone, "How are you?" they reply, "I'm fine" or "I'm OK." But one lazy Monday afternoon recently a new colleague of mine replied, "Oh, I am fabulous!" It made me smile, so I asked him what was making him feel so fabulous and he said, "I'm healthy, my family is healthy, and we live in a free country. So I don't have any reason not to be happy." The difference was simply his attitude and his choice of words. He wasn't necessarily any better off than anyone else, but he seemed twenty times happier. Spend the next thirty days using words that encourage a smile.

2. Try one new thing every day.

Variety truly is the spice of life. You can see or do something a million times, but you can only see or do it for the first time once. As a result, first-time experiences often leave reflective marks in our minds for the rest of our lives. Make an effort to try something new every day for the next thirty days. It can be a whole new activity or just a small experience, such as talking to a stranger. Once you get the ball rolling, many of these new experiences will open doors to life-changing opportunities.

3. Perform one selfless act every day.

In life, you get what you put in. When you make a positive impact on someone else's life, you also make a positive impact on your own life. Do something that's greater than you, something that helps someone else be happy or suffer less. I promise, it will be an extremely rewarding experience. One you'll likely remember forever. Obviously your options here are limitless, but if you're looking to assist an ordinary person in need without leaving your chair, check out the GoFundMe website.

4. Learn and practice one new skill every day.

Self-reliance is a vital key to living a healthy, productive life. To be self-reliant, one must master a basic set of skills, more or less making them a jack-of-all-trades. Contrary to what you may have learned in school, a jack-of-all-trades is far better equipped to deal with life than a specialized master of only one. And besides, learning new skills is fun.

5. Teach someone something new every day.

We all have natural strengths and talents that can dramatically help those around us. What comes easy for you is no doubt challenging for others. We tend to take these gifts for granted, often hardly noticing what we have to offer, and thus we rarely share them with others. Inner happiness and zeal come from using these inherent gifts on a routine basis. What do people thank you for? What do people routinely ask for your help with? Most people's passions and talents help others in one way or another. Perhaps for you it's painting, teaching math, cooking a good meal, or leading an exercise class. For the next thirty days, devote some time each day to sharing your talents and expertise.

6. Dedicate an hour a day to something you're passionate about.

Take part in something you passionately believe in. This could be anything. Some people take an active role in their city council, some find refuge in religious faith, some join social clubs supporting causes they believe in, and others find passion in their hobbies. In each case the psychological outcome is the same. They engage themselves in something they strongly believe in. This engagement brings happiness and meaning into their lives.

7. Treat everyone nicely, even those who are rude to you.

Being nice to someone you dislike doesn't mean you're fake. It means you're mature enough to control your emotions. Treat everyone with kindness and respect, even those who are rude to you—not because they're nice, but because you are. Do this for thirty days and I guarantee you'll see the rudeness around you dissipate.

8. Concentrate on being positive at all times.

The real winners in life cultivate optimism. They have the ability to manufacture their own happiness and drive. No matter what the situation, the successful diva is the woman who will always find a way to put an optimistic spin on it. She knows failure only as an opportunity to grow and learn a new lesson from life. People who think optimistically see the world as a place packed with endless opportunities, especially in trying times. Try to spend the next thirty days looking at the bright side of things.

9. Address and acknowledge the lesson in inconvenient situations.

It's important to remember that everything is a life lesson. Everyone you meet, everything you encounter—they're all part of the learning experience we call "life." Never forget to acknowledge the lesson, especially when things don't go your way. If you don't get a job you wanted or a relationship doesn't work, it only means something better is out there waiting. And the lesson you just learned is the first step toward it. Over the next thirty days, keep a written log of all the lessons life has taught you.

10. Pay attention and enjoy your life as it happens.

When I watched the Academy Awards recently, I realized that most of the speeches actors and actresses make when they accept an award go something like this: "This means so much to me. My whole life has been leading up to this moment." But the truth is, our whole lives have been leading up to every moment. Think about that for a second. Every single thing you've gone through in life, every high, every low, and everything in between, has led you to this moment right now. Ask yourself this: How much of life are you actually living? If you're like most people, the answer is likely: "Not enough." The key is to concentrate a little less on doing and a little more on being. Remember, right now is the only moment guaranteed to you. Right now is life. Spend the next thirty days living in the now, for real.

11. Get rid of one thing a day for thirty days.

We have so much clutter surrounding us at any given moment (at the office, in our cars, in our homes) and we've become so accustomed to it that we no longer notice how it affects us. If you start cleaning up some of this external clutter, a lot of internal clutter will disappear as well. Choose one needless item every day and get rid of it. It's that simple. It might be difficult at first, so expect some resistance. But after some time you will begin to learn to let go of your pack rat tendencies, and your mind will thank you for your efforts.

12. Create something brand-new in thirty days or less.

Creation is a process like none other. Putting to use your innovative faculties and constructing something with your own two hands will leave you with an indescribable sense of wholeness. There is no substitute for it. The only caveat is that it must be related to something you actually care about. If you are creating financial plans for clients all day and you hate it, that doesn't really count. But if you can find something you love, and create something related to it, it will make all the difference in your life. If you haven't created something in a while just for the sake of creating, do so. Take the next thirty days and let your creativity run wild.

13. Don't tell a single lie for thirty days.

With all the seemingly innocent white lies that trickle out of us, this is way harder than it sounds. But you can do it. Stop deceiving yourself and others, speak from the heart, speak the whole truth.

14. Wake up thirty minutes early every morning.

Get up thirty minutes earlier than usual so you don't have to rush around like a maniac. Those thirty minutes will help you avoid speeding tickets, tardiness, and other stressors. Give it a legitimate try for thirty days straight and see how it impacts your life.

15. Ditch three bad habits for thirty days.

Do you eat too much fast food? Do you play too many video games? Do you argue with your siblings? You know some of your bad habits. Pick three and quit doing them for thirty days. Period.

16. Watch less than thirty minutes of TV every day.

Entertain yourself with real-world experiences. Great memories are the product of interesting life experiences. So turn off the television (or the computer if that's how you watch your TV programs) and get outdoors. Interact with the world, appreciate nature, take notice of the simple pleasures life has to offer, and just watch as life unfolds in front of you.

17. Define one long-term goal and work on it for an hour every day.

Break your goal down into bite-sized pieces and focus on achieving one piece at a time. It really is all about taking baby steps, and taking the first step is often the hardest. Spend an hour every day for the next thirty days working toward something you've always wanted to accomplish. Take a small dream and make it a reality.

18. Read one chapter of a good book every day.

With the Web's endless stream of informative, easy-to-skim textual snippets and collaborative written works, people are spending more and more time reading online. Nevertheless, the Web cannot replace the authoritative wisdom from certain classic books that have delivered (or will deliver) profound ideas around the globe for generations. Books open doors, in your mind and in your life. Read an online book list and find a good book to grab at the library today. Then spend the next thirty days reading at least one chapter a day until you reach the end.

19. Every morning, watch or read something that inspires you.

Sometimes all you need is a little pep talk. For the next thirty days, before you eat breakfast or leave the house, watch a motivational video or read something (quotation, blog post, short story) that inspires you.

20. Do something every day after lunch that makes you laugh.

Watch a funny video clip on YouTube, read your favorite comic strip, or find a good joke online. A good chuckle stimulates the mind and can give you a renewed level of energy. The best time for this laugh is during the lull in the midafternoon, when you need it most.

21. Go alcohol- and drug-free for thirty days.

This challenge depends on your individual circumstance. If you are a heavy user of alcohol or a particular drug, it is not recommended that you quit cold turkey. You need to see a physician and ease off of the substance slowly. But if you are a casual user, quit right now for thirty days.

22. Exercise for thirty minutes every day for thirty days.

Your health is your life. Don't let it go. Eat right, exercise, and get an annual physical checkup.

23. Get uncomfortable and face a fear every day.

With a strategy of continuous small steps into uncomfortable territory, we are often able to sidestep the biggest barrier to positive change: fear. Sometimes we're afraid we'll fail. Sometimes we're subconsciously afraid we'll succeed and then we'd have to deal with all the disruption (growth) and change that follows success. And other times it's our fear of rejection or simply our fear of looking like a fool. The best way to defeat fear is to stare it down. Connect to your fear, feel it in your body, realize it, and steadily address it. Greet it by name if you have to: "Welcome, fear." Fear can be a guiding friend if you learn how to swallow it, and listen to it only when it serves its true purpose of warning you when you are in danger. Spend an hour every day for the next thirty days addressing a fear that is holding you back.

24. Cook one new, healthful recipe every day.

Cooking is fun, challenges your mind, and if done correctly, provides vital nutrients to your body. Win–win–win. *How to Cook Everything* by

Mark Bittman is a great tool for this challenge. Packed with nine hundred pages of simple instructions on how to cook everything you could ever dream of eating, it's pretty much the greatest cookbook ever written. Prepare one new, healthful recipe every day for the next thirty days.

25. Spend ten minutes every evening reflecting on what went well.

For the next thirty days, spend ten minutes every evening pondering the small successes that occurred during the course of the day. This process of positive reflection will remind you of all the tiny blessings in your life, and help you to celebrate your personal growth.

26. Have a conversation every day with someone you rarely speak to.

People are interesting creatures, and no two people are exactly alike. Interacting with different people will open your mind to fascinating ideas and perspectives. So for the next thirty days, strike up a conversation with someone you rarely speak to, or someone you've never met before. Find out what makes them tick.

27. Pay down debt and don't create any new debt for thirty days.

Live well below your means. Don't buy stuff you don't need. Sleep on big purchases. Create a budget and savings plan and stick to them. For the next thirty days, pay for things in cash and micromanage every cent you make and spend.

28. Let go of one relationship that constantly hurts you.

Keep people in your life who truly love you, motivate you, encourage you, enhance you, and make you happy. If you know people who do none of these things, let them go and make room for new positive relationships. Over the next thirty days, if relevant to your situation, gradually let go of one person in your life who has been continuously hurting you and holding you back.

29. Publicly forgive someone who deserves another chance.

Sometimes good relationships end abruptly because of big egos and arguments based on isolated incidents. If there's someone in your life who truly deserves another chance, give it to them. If you need to apologize too, do it. Over the next thirty days, give your story together a new chapter.

30. Document every day with one photograph and one paragraph.

For thirty days, bring a camera with you wherever you go. Do your best to take one photograph that represents a standout experience from each day. Then, before you go to bed each night, write one paragraph in a notebook or journal that highlights your day. If you do it all digitally, you can unite your daily photograph and paragraph in one digital space (like a personal blog), which can be easily reviewed in the future. Many moons from now these old photos and journal entries will ignite your recollection of interesting memories you would have otherwise forgotten.

AS YOU PROGRESS through these challenges, remember that personal growth is a slow, steady process. It can't be rushed. You need to work on it gradually every day. There is ample time for you to be who you want to be in life. Don't settle for less than what you think you deserve, or less than you know you can be. Despite the struggles you'll face along the way, never give up on yourself. You're braver than you believe, stronger than you seem, smarter than you think, and twice as capable as you have ever imagined.

10 THINGS You Must GIVE UP to Be Successful

WHEN WE THINK about how to achieve success, we often focus on the skills and habits we should add to our lives. But sometimes the key to success actually lies in our ability to give up certain habits and behaviors. So starting today . . .

1. Give up the habit of waiting.

The way you spend your time defines who you are. You don't get to choose how you are going to die, or when; you can only decide how you are going to live right now. Trust me, a year from now you will wish you had started today.

2. Give up the excuses.

Sooner or later you will come to realize that it's not what you lose along the way that counts, it's what you do with what you still have. When you let go, forgive, and move on, you in no way change the past, you change the future.

3. Give up trying to be perfect.

The beauty of each of us lies in our vulnerability, our love, our complex emotions—our authentic imperfections. When we embrace who we are and decide to be authentic instead of perfect, we open ourselves up to real relationships, real happiness, and real success. There is no need to put on a mask. There is no need to pretend to be someone you're not. You are perfectly imperfect just the way you are.

4. Give up doing things you know are wrong.

Nothing is more damaging to you than doing something that you believe is wrong. Your beliefs alone don't help you grow and thrive, your behavior and actions do. So always do what you know in your heart is right for you.

5. Give up feelings of entitlement.

Nobody owes you anything. When you approach life with the false sense that you are owed things, you will naturally become less productive and constantly find yourself disappointed by reality. When you are grateful for what you have, and see positive things as bonuses rather than owed entitlements, you will earn great successes gradually as you grow.

6. Give up relationships that want you to be someone else.

The best kind of relationship is the one that makes you a better person without changing you into someone other than yourself.

7. Give up letting others decide what you can and can't do.

In order to live your own authentic life, you have to follow *your* inner GPS, not someone else's. When others say, "You can't do it!" or "That's impossible," don't lose hope. Just because they couldn't doesn't mean you can't.

8. Give up being a helpless victim.

Yes, it is unfortunate that sometimes bad things happen to the best of people. Life can be unfair, unkind, and unjust. However, being stuck in a victim mentality does not nurture your ability to move onward and upward. You've got to stand back up and take positive steps to heal and grow.

9. Give up worrying about past failures.

Accept your past without regret, handle your present with confidence, and face your future without fear. You are today where your thoughts and actions have brought you; you will be tomorrow where your thoughts and actions take you.

10. Give up blaming everyone else.

Either you own your situation or it will own you. Either you take responsibility for your life or someone else will. Blame is a scapegoat—it's an easy way out of taking accountability for your own outcome. It's a lot easier to point the finger at someone or something else instead of looking within. Blame is not constructive; it does not help you or anyone else—nobody wins in the blame game. The amount of energy and stress it takes to place blame elsewhere takes away from your ability to move forward and find a real solution.

And remember, the road you are traveling may be the more challenging one, but don't lose faith. Don't listen to the doubters, don't let setbacks keep you down, and most of all, don't give up on yourself.

It's OK if you don't know how much more you can handle. It's fine if you don't know exactly what to do next. Eventually you'll let go of how things "should be" and start to see all the great possibilities in front of you. This is your life—grab the wheel with both hands and keep steering yourself in the right direction.

10 SUCCESS Principles
We Often Forget

SOMETIMES WE FIND ourselves running in place, struggling to get ahead simply because we forget to address some of the basic success principles that govern our potential to make progress. So here's a quick reminder:

1. You are the only person responsible for your success.

The best part of your life will start on the day you decide your life is your own—no one to lean on, rely on, or blame. You are in full control of your future. Believe with all your heart that you will do what you were made to do. It may be tough at times, but refuse to follow some pre-ordained path. Make your own rules and have your own game plan. There is no happiness and success to be found by playing it safe and settling for a life that is less than the one you are capable of living.

2. You don't have to reinvent the wheel.

Actually, to be successful you don't have to invent anything at all. Coming up with a new invention or idea is one way to achieve massive success, but it isn't necessary. And it can be the most challenging road to success there is. You see, many people have found lots of success just by taking something that already existed and simply putting their own twist on it (their unique selling proposition). Connecting things means seeking inspiration from great ideas that already exist and adding your own useful twist.

3. There is no progress without action.

What is not started today is never finished tomorrow. Some of the greatest ideas never made it. Why? Because the genius behind the idea failed to take action. Just remember, no action always results in a 100 percent failure rate. So get into action now, and begin to move in the right direction. Once you get started, every step afterward gets easier and easier, until eventually what had once been invisible starts to become visible, and what once felt unattainable starts to become a reality.

4. Persistence always wins.

It may take more than one swing to develop an efficient hit, so make sure not to give up on strike one. And remember, a river cuts through rocks not because of its power at a given moment, but because of its persistence over time.

5. Focus is everything.

When you are too busy looking behind and around you, people are passing you. If you never focus clearly on something, you will never be 100 percent efficient at anything. Multitasking might seem to make you efficient at getting multiple tasks done at once, but it usually reduces your efficiency in dealing with each individual task.

6. Failure is necessary.

Don't wake up at seventy-five years of age sighing over what you should have tried but didn't, because you were afraid to fail. Just do it, and be willing to fail and learn along the way. Very few people get it right the first time. In fact, most people fail to get it right the first five times. If what you did today didn't turn out as you hoped, tomorrow is a new opportunity to do it differently. Interpret each failure as a lesson on the road to success.

7. Positivity fuels productivity.

Thoughts are like the steering wheel that moves our life in the right direction. Success comes from positive energy. You can choose to get caught up in the negativity surrounding you, or you can decide to do something positive about your situation. You always have a choice. Remember, happiness is an element of success, and the happiest people don't necessarily have the best of everything; they use positive energy to make the best of what they have.

8. You must believe you can.

You must find the place inside yourself where anything is possible. It starts with a dream. Add confidence, and it becomes a belief. Add commitment, and it becomes a goal in sight. Add action, and it becomes a part of your life. Add determination and time, and your dream becomes a reality.

9. Helping others is a big part of being successful.

Successful people constantly come up with new ideas, new projects, and new and innovative ways of helping others. This means that your aims and objectives benefit you, but also help benefit others as well. Bottom line: Your long-term success is directly tied to how well you serve your community.

10. Success is a journey of countless baby steps.

It's a constant process of growth. If you want to be successful, you must continue to hold yourself to a higher standard than anyone else, and strive to improve. Oftentimes a person or organization will be successful but then drop off. A person may become lazy, and an organization may succumb to weaknesses or competition. Sustained success means continually improving even if others may not see a need for it. Remember, the great thing in the world is not so much where we stand at any given time, as it is in what direction we are moving.

20 QUESTIONS You Should Ask Yourself Every Sunday

AT THE CUSP of new beginnings, many of us take time to reflect on our lives by looking back over the past and ahead into the future. We ponder the successes, failures, and standout events that are slowly scripting our life's story. This process of self-reflection helps us maintain a conscious awareness of where we've been and where we intend to go. It is pertinent to the organization and preservation of our dreams, goals, and desires.

If you would like to maximize the benefits of self-reflection, I have twenty questions for you. These questions should be reviewed every Sunday morning or sometime during the weekend when you have some quiet time to think. Remember, reflection is the key to progression.

1. *What did I learn last week?*

2. *What was my greatest accomplishment over the past week?*

3. *Which moment from last week was the most memorable and why?*

4. *What's the number one thing I need to accomplish this week?*

5. *What can I do right now to make the week less stressful?*

6. *What have I struggled with in the past that might also affect the upcoming week?*

7. *What was last week's biggest time sink?*

8. *Am I carrying any excess baggage into the upcoming week that can be dropped?*

9. *What have I been avoiding that needs to get done?*

10. *What opportunities are still on the table?*

11. *Is there anyone I've been meaning to talk to?*

12. *Is there anyone that deserves a big "thank you"?*

13. *How can I help someone else this coming week?*

14. *What are my top three goals for the next three years?*

15. *Have any of my recent actions moved me closer to my goals?*

16. *What's the next step for each goal?*

17. *What am I looking forward to during the upcoming week?*

18. *What are my fears?*

19. *What am I most grateful for?*

20. *If I knew I only had one week to live, who would I spend my time with?*

TAKE THIRTY MINUTES every Sunday and give yourself the gift of self-reflection. It has worked wonders for us, and we're confident it will do the same for you.

HOW TO ACHIEVE
THE IMPOSSIBLE

The impossible is what nobody can do until somebody does.

TELEPORTATION IS THE new air travel. Humans can walk on water. And there is a cure for cancer. These things will happen eventually because, quite simply, the nature of progression dictates that they must happen. And because there are people on this planet who believe they can make them happen.

Are you one of these people?

3 Short Stories on Achieving the Impossible

When I was a high school freshman, a 260-pound freshman girl showed up for track-and-field tryouts. Her name was Sara, and she was only there because her doctor said her health depended on it. But once she scanned the crowd of students who were trying out, she turned around and began walking away. Coach O'Leary saw her, jogged over, and turned her back around. "I'm not thin enough for this sport!" Sara declared. "And I'll never be! It's impossible for me to lose enough weight. I've tried." Coach O'Leary nodded, and promised Sara that her body type wasn't suited for her current weight. "It's suited for 220 pounds," he said. Sara looked confused. "Most people tell me I need to lose 130 pounds," she replied. "But you think I only need to lose 40?" Coach O'Leary nodded again. Sara started off as a shot-put competitor, but spent every single afternoon running and training with the rest of the track team. She was very competitive, and by the end of our freshman year she was down to 220 pounds. She also won second place in the countywide shot-put tournament that year. Three years later, during our senior year, she won third place in the 10K run. Her competitive weight at the time was 130 pounds.

When Charles Darwin wrote *On the Origin of Species*, which proposed the groundbreaking idea of evolution by natural selection, it launched a worldwide debate. Supporters included scientists, historians, and others whose professions and worldviews required that they carefully analyze new ideas and adopt those that seemed to make sense. Critics included theologians, conservative extremists, and others who were convinced that the biblical explanation of our ancestry was the only possible explanation. This group of people, the ones who refused to accept the possibility of new ideas, eventually alienated themselves from the debate, and arguably failed to assist in the progression of mankind. The people who didn't blindly reject evolution, who instead questioned it, researched it, and sought to explore its possibilities, were able to achieve previously impossible feats by making important advances in various fields of study from sociology to history to medicine.

When Sergey Brin and Larry Page founded Google, they had absolutely no intention of building the most powerful Internet-based company in the world. In the mid-1990s, the Internet was already saturated with many established search engine companies such as Yahoo, Lycos, and AltaVista. Competing and succeeding in such a competitive environment seemed impossible to them. So instead, they tried to sell their search technology to these companies. And although Google, with its

PageRank algorithm and efficient scaling, was clearly more cutting-edge than any search technology currently in place, none of these established companies wanted to get their hands dirty with Google's new technology. So after exhausting their options, Brin and Page decided to release Google to the public and directly compete with the biggest names in the business. As we know, they blew them out of the water.

"Impossible" Is Simply a State of Mind

If we can find the patience to see the world for what it is—dynamic, flexible, and loaded with untapped potential—and if we can accept the fact that change is an inevitable and brilliant part of life, then we can partake in the thrill of progression and help shape a world in which the impossible becomes possible.

To achieve the impossible, we must first understand that the "state of impossible" is simply a "state of mind." Nothing is truly impossible. Impossibility only exists when we lack the proper knowledge and experience to comprehend how something can be possible.

Sara was convinced that it was impossible to lose weight because, in her past experience, it had never worked out the way she had hoped. Nineteenth-century theologians laughed at Charles Darwin's theories because his theories didn't come from the Bible, which, at the time, was their sole source of knowledge and truth. Google's old competitors didn't recognize the next big thing when it was offered to them on a silver platter. Why? Because they didn't want to bother with a new technology that they didn't fully understand. This ultimately forced Google's Brin and Page to achieve their version of the "impossible."

So let's start training our minds and our hearts, today, so we can turn today's impossibility into tomorrow's reality.

SUCCESS QUESTIONS
TO MAKE YOU THINK

What's the number one thing you want to ACHIEVE in the *next five* years?

If we learn from our MISTAKES, why are we always so *afraid* to make a mistake?

What's something that used to SCARE you, but *no longer* does?

What MISTAKE do you *make* over and over again?

What did FEAR of *failure* stop you from doing?

If you could LEARN *anything*, what would it be?

What is something you will CONTINUE to do until the day you *die*?

What is the best ADVICE you have ever *received*?

If I were to say to you, "JUST GO FOR IT," what would "*it*" be?

What's something you must GIVE UP to *move forward*?

PART EIGHT

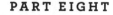

Simplicity

Life is not complicated. We are complicated.
When we stop doing the wrong things and start doing
the right things, life becomes simple.

WHAT WE WANT TO BE WHEN WE GROW UP

WHEN I WAS in elementary school, my parents told me it didn't matter what I did when I grew up, so long as it made me happy. "Happiness is the whole point of life," my father said. "Your mother loves to help people, so she became a nurse. I love reading, writing, and poetry, so I became an English teacher. We both find happiness in the work we do each day."

A few years later when I was in junior high, my grumpy sixth-grade homeroom teacher put me in detention for "being difficult": She went around the classroom and asked each student what they wanted to be when they grew up. When she got to me, I told her I wanted to be happy. She told me I was missing the whole point of the question. I told her she was missing the whole point of life.

What do we all want to be when we grow up? Happy . . . that is all. Find what makes you happy and do it until you die.

12 THINGS You Should Be Able to SAY About Yourself

YOU KNOW YOU'RE on the right track when you can repeat each of the following to yourself, honestly. (And if you can't, this list gives you something positive to work on.)

1. I am following my heart and intuition.

Don't be pushed by your problems. Be led by your dreams. Live the life you want to live. Be the person you want to remember years from now. Make decisions and act on them. Make mistakes, fall, and try again. Even if you fall a thousand times, at least you won't have to wonder what could have been. At least you will know in your heart that you gave your dreams your best shot.

2. I am proud of myself.

You are your own best friend and your own biggest critic. Regardless of the opinions of others, at the end of the day the only reflection staring back at you in the mirror is your own. Accept everything about yourself—*everything!* You are you and that is the beginning and the end—no apologies, no regrets.

3. I am making a difference.

Act as if what you do makes a difference. It does. You are only one, but you are one. You cannot do everything, but you can do something. Smile and enjoy the fact that you made a difference—one you'll likely remember forever.

4. I am happy and grateful.

Happiness is within you, in your way of thinking. How you view yourself and your world are mindful choices and habits. The lens you choose to view everything through determines how you feel about yourself and everything that happens around you.

5. I am growing into the best version of me.

Wearing a mask wears you out. Faking it is fatiguing. The most arduous activity is pretending to be what you know you aren't. Trying to fit some idealistic mold of perfection is a fool's game. It's much wiser to just be yourself—faults and all. Improve continuously, take care of your body and health, and surround yourself with positivity. Become the best version of you.

6. I am making my time count.

Remember, your time is priceless, but it's free. You can't own it, but you can use it. You can spend it, but you can't keep it. Once you've lost it, you can never get it back. You really do only have a short period to live. So let your dreams be bigger than your fears, and your actions louder than your words. Make your time count!

7. I am honest with myself.

Be honest about what's right, as well as what needs to be changed. Be honest about what you want to achieve and who you want to become. Be honest with every aspect of your life, always. Because you are the one person you can forever count on.

8. I am good to those I care about.

When was the last time you told your family and close personal friends that you loved them? Just spending a little time with someone shows that you care, shows that they are important enough that you've chosen—out of all the things to do on your busy schedule—to find the time for them. Talk to them. Listen to them. Understand them. Many times it's our actions, not just our words, that really speak what our heart feels for another.

9. I know what unconditional love feels like.

Whether your love is toward a child, a lover, or another family member, know the feeling of giving love and not expecting anything in return—this is what lies at the heart of unconditional love. Life through unconditional love is a wondrous adventure that excites the very core of our being and lights our path with delight. This love is a dynamic and powerful energy that lifts us through the most difficult times.

10. I have forgiven those who once hurt me.

Grudges are a waste of perfect happiness, causing us to miss out on the beauty of life as it happens. To forgive is to set yourself free.

11. I take full accountability for my life.

You are the only one who can directly control the outcome of your life. And no, it won't always be easy. Every person has a stack of obstacles in front of them. But you must take accountability for your situation and overcome these obstacles. Choosing not to is choosing a lifetime of mere existence.

12. I have no regrets.

This one is simply a culmination of the previous eleven . . . Follow your heart. Be true to yourself. Do what makes you happy. Be with who makes you smile. Laugh as much as you breathe. Love as long as you live. Say what you need to say. Offer a helping hand when you're able. Appreciate all the things you do have. Smile. Celebrate your small victories. Learn from your mistakes. Realize that everything is a lesson in disguise. Forgive. And let go of the things you can't control.

12 AMAZINGLY
Achievable Things
to Do Today

"**WHAT CAN I** start doing today to make my life happier and more rewarding?" This is the most common question readers ask us via e-mail, Facebook, and Twitter. So we dug into our archives and came up with a list of twelve simple, actionable ways to improve your well-being on a daily basis. Starting today . . .

1. Smile.

A smile is a choice, not a miracle. Don't wait for people to smile. Show them how. A genuine smile makes you and everyone around you feel better. The simple act of smiling sends a message to your brain that you're happy. And when you're happy, your body pumps out all kinds of feel-good endorphins. This reaction has been studied and proven a number of times. Bottom line: Smiling actually makes you happier.

2. Treat everyone with kindness and respect.

Remember, there are no boundaries or classes that define a group of people who deserve to be respected. Treat everyone with the same level of respect you would give to your grandfather and the same level of patience you would have with your baby brother. People will notice your kindness.

3. Perform one selfless act.

In life, you get what you put in. When you make a positive impact in someone else's life, you also make a positive impact in your own life. Do something that's greater than you, something that helps someone else be happy or suffer less. I promise, it will be an extremely rewarding experience. One you'll likely remember forever.

4. Avoid needless drama and those who create it.

Never create unnecessary drama, and don't surround yourself with those who do. Choose to spend time with people you are proud to know, people you admire, who love and respect you—people who make your day a little brighter simply by being in it. Don't walk away from negative people, *run!* Life is too short to spend time with folks who suck the happiness out of you.

5. Think of the positives.

Stop being afraid of what could go wrong, and start thinking of what could go right. Better yet, think of everything that already is right. Be thankful for nights that turned into mornings, friends who turned into family, and past dreams and goals that turned into realities. And use this positivity to fuel an even brighter tomorrow.

6. Inject a little love into the world around you.

Love what you are doing, until you can do what you love. Love where you are, until you can be where you love. Love the people you are with, until you can be with the people you love most. This is the way we find happiness.

7. Take decisive and immediate action on a decision that needs to be made.

As we grow older and wiser, we begin to understand what we need and what we need to leave behind. Sometimes walking away is a step forward. Sometimes it's better to let go without closure. Actions and behavior speak volumes. Trust the signs you were given, and take the next step.

8. Follow your intuition when making decisions.

Following your intuition means doing what feels right, even if it doesn't look or sound right to others. Only time will tell, but our human instincts are rarely ever wrong. So don't worry about what everyone else thinks, and keep living and speaking your truth. The only people who will get mad at you for doing so are those who are set on living a lie.

9. Spend time working on something you believe in.

Never put off or give up on a goal that's important to you. Not because you still have tomorrow to start or try again, but because you may not have tomorrow at all. Life is shorter than it sometimes seems. Follow your heart today.

10. Meet someone new.

Most humans have a habit of stagnating in a small circle of friends, but it doesn't help us grow. Get out there and meet new people. You'll be surprised at the lessons they will teach you and the new opportunities they will inject into your life.

11. Exercise and eat healthfully.

Taking care of your body is crucial to being the happiest person you can be. If you don't have your physical energy in good shape, then your mental energy (your focus), your emotional energy (your feelings), and your spiritual energy (your purpose) will all be negatively affected. Those who exercise have a higher sense of self-accomplishment and self-worth.

12. Be a student of life.

Experience it, learn from it, and absorb all the knowledge you can. Prepare yourself for greatness by keeping your mind conditioned with fresh knowledge and new challenges. Remember, if you stay ready, you don't have to get ready when great opportunities arise.

10 AFFIRMATIONS for a Good Life

A GOOD LIFE is when you assume nothing, do more, need less, smile often, and realize how fortunate you are right now. It's about the simple pleasures that make you happy, the compassionate deeds you perform, the personal goals you strive to achieve, the relationships you nurture, and the legacy you leave behind.

So starting today, choose to take control. Here are ten affirmations to help you live a good life:

1. *I am not perfect and I will not try to be.*

2. *I cannot, and will not try to, please everyone.*

3. *I will take part in something I believe in.*

4. *I will prioritize my obligations and do important things first.*

5. *I will choose my friends wisely.*

6. *I will help others when I am able.*

7. *I will focus on the positive.*

8. *I can only be me.*

9. *I will be here now.*

10. *Life gets better when I decide to move forward.*

The world around you changes when you change.

If you awake every morning with the thought that something wonderful will happen in your life today, and you pay close attention, you'll often find that you're right. The opposite is also true. The choice is yours to make.

12 RULES for Being Human

DON'T TRY TO be perfect. Just be an excellent example of being human. Here are a few things to keep in mind:

1. Growth requires pain.

Don't be afraid to fall apart for a little while. Because when it happens, the situation will open an opportunity for you to grow and rebuild yourself into the brilliant person you are capable of being.

2. You will learn as long as you live.

There is no stage of life that does not contain new lessons. And as long as you follow your heart and never stop learning, you'll turn not older, but newer every day.

3. There is a positive lesson in every life experience.

Don't forget to acknowledge the lesson, especially when things don't go your way. If you make a mistake that sets you back a little, or a business deal or a relationship doesn't work, it only means a new opportunity is out there waiting. And the lesson you just learned is the first step toward it.

4. True beauty lives under the skin.

When you start to really know someone, most of their physical characteristics vanish in your mind. You begin to dwell in their energy, recognize their scent, and appreciate their wit. You see only the essence of the person, not the shell. And that's why, when you really connect with a person's inner self, most physical imperfections become irrelevant.

5. Only you know what you're capable of.

Unless someone can look into the core of your heart and see the degree of your passion, or look into the depths of your soul and see the extent of your will, then they have no business telling you what you can or cannot achieve. Because while they may know the odds, they do not know *you*, and what you're capable of.

6. Your love creates your happiness.

The happiness you feel is in direct proportion to the love you give. When you love, you subconsciously strive to become better than you are. When you strive to become better than you are, everything around you becomes better too. During your youth, love will be your teacher; in your middle age, love will be your foundation; and in your old age, love will be your fondest memories and your greatest delight.

7. You earn respect by being respectful.

You earn respect by listening, acknowledging feelings, and treating others with the same respect you hope to get in return. So treat people the way you want to be treated. Talk to people the way you want to be talked to. Respect is earned, not given.

8. Negativity poisons the soul.

Don't let needless drama and negativity stop you from being the best you can be. Avoid the drama, and focus on what truly matters. Let go of the things that are weighing you down. As you unclutter your life, you will slowly free yourself to answer the callings of your inner spirit.

9. Your health is your life.

To truly be your best, you must give your body the fuel it needs. Toss the junk and fill your kitchen with fresh, whole foods. Run, swim, bike, walk—sweat! Good health is essential for having the energy, stamina, and outlook to tackle your goals and dreams.

10. Letting go is part of moving on to something better.

You will not get what you truly deserve if you're too attached to the things you're supposed to let go of. Sometimes you love, and you struggle, and you learn, and you move on. And that's OK. You must be willing to let go of the life you planned for so you can enjoy the life that is waiting for you.

11. This moment is a gift.

The truth is, your whole life has been leading up to this moment. Think about that for a second. Every single thing you've gone through in life, every high, every low, and everything in between, has led you to this moment right now. This moment is priceless, and it's the only moment guaranteed to you. This moment is your "life." Don't miss it.

12. Your choices design your life.

You have a choice every single day. Choose to appreciate what you have. Choose to make time for yourself. Choose to do something that makes you smile. Choose to be excited. Choose to laugh at your own silliness. Choose to spend time with positive people. Choose to be persistent with your goals. Choose to try again and again. Within your choices lie all the tools and resources you need to design the life of your dreams; it's just a matter of choosing wisely.

10 SIMPLE Truths That Smart People Forget

SOME OF THE smartest people we know continuously struggle to get ahead because they forget to address a few simple truths that collectively govern our potential to make progress. So here's a quick reminder:

1. Education and intelligence accomplish nothing without action.

There's a huge difference between knowing how to do something and actually doing it. Knowledge and intelligence are both useless without action.

2. Happiness and success are two different things.

"What will make me happy?" and "What will make me successful?" are two of the most important questions you can ask yourself. But they are two different questions.

3. Everyone runs their own business.

No matter how you make a living or who you think you work for, you only work for one person, yourself. The big question is: What are you selling, and to whom? Even when you have a full-time, salaried, "Corporate America" position, you are still running your own business. So how can you simultaneously save your time and increase your profit? The answer is slightly different for everyone. But it's an answer you should be seeking.

4. Having too many choices interferes with decision making.

Here in the twenty-first century, where information moves at the speed of light and opportunities for innovation seem endless, we have an abundant array of choices when it comes to designing our lives and careers. But sadly, an abundance of choice often leads to indecision, confusion, and inaction.

So if you're trying to make a decision, don't waste all your time evaluating every last detail of every possible option. Choose something that you think will work and give it a shot. If it doesn't work out, choose something else and keep pressing forward.

5. All people possess dimensions of success and dimensions of failure.

Trying to be perfect is a waste of time and energy. Perfection is an illusion.

All people, even our heroes, are multidimensional. Powerful business people, polished musicians, best-selling authors, and even our own parents all have dimensions of success and dimensions of failure present in their lives.

Our successful dimensions usually encompass the things we spend the most time doing. We are successful in these dimensions because of our prolonged commitment to them. This is the part of our lives we want others to see—the successful part that holds our life's work. It's the notion of putting our best foot forward. It's the public persona we envision as our personal legacy: "The Successful ABC" or "The Award-Winning XYZ."

But behind whichever polished story line we outwardly promote, there lies a multidimensional human being with a long list of unprofessed failures. Sometimes this person is a bad husband or wife. Sometimes this person laughs at the expense of others. And sometimes this person merely takes their eyes off the road and rear-ends the car in front of them.

6. Every mistake you make is progress.

Mistakes teach you important lessons. Every time you make one, you're one step closer to your goal. The only mistake that can truly hurt you is choosing to do nothing simply because you're too scared to make a mistake.

So don't hesitate—don't doubt yourself. In life, it's rarely about getting a chance, it's about taking a chance. If you never act, you will never know for sure, and you will be left standing in the same spot forever. The truth is that we all fail. The greater truth is that no single failure ever defines us. Confess. Apologize. Learn. Grow wiser. Press on.

7. People can be great at doing things they don't like to do.

Although we're not suggesting that you choose a career or trade you dislike, we've heard way too many smart people say something like, "In order to be great at what you do, you have to like what you do." This just isn't true.

A good friend of ours is a public accountant. He has told us on numerous occasions that he dislikes his job—that it "bores him to death." But he frequently gets raises and promotions. At the age of twenty-eight, out of nearly a thousand junior accountants in his division, he's one of only two who were promoted to be senior accountants this past year. Why? Because even though he doesn't like doing it, he's good at what he does.

We could come up with dozens of other examples just like this, but we'll spare you the details. Just realize that if someone dedicates enough time and attention to perfecting a skill or trade, they can be insanely good at it as a side hustle, a weekend gig, or simply doing something they don't like to do.

8. The problems we have with others are typically more about us.

Quite often, the problems we have with others—our spouse, parents, siblings—don't really have much to do with them at all. Because many of the problems we think we have with them we subconsciously created in our own mind. Maybe they did something in the past that touched on one of our fears or insecurities. Or maybe they didn't do something that we expected them to do. In either case, problems like these are not about the other person, they're about us.

And that's OK. It simply means these little predicaments will be easier to solve. We are, after all, in charge of our own decisions. We get to decide whether we want to keep our head cluttered with events from the past, or instead open our minds to the positive realities unfolding in front of us.

All we need is the willingness to look at things a little differently—letting go of "what was" and "what should have been," and instead focusing our energy on "what is" and "what could be possible."

9. Emotional decisions are rarely good decisions.

Decisions driven by heavy emotion are typically misguided reactions rather than educated judgments. These reactions are the by-product of minimal amounts of conscious thought and primarily based on momentary "feelings" instead of mindful awareness.

The best advice here is simple: Don't let your emotions trump your intelligence. Slow down and think things through before you make any life-changing decisions.

10. You will never feel 100 percent ready when an opportunity arises.

The number one thing I persistently see holding smart people back is their own reluctance to accept an opportunity simply because they don't think they're ready. In other words, they believe they require additional knowledge, skill, experience, and so on before they can aptly partake in the opportunity. Sadly, this is the kind of thinking that stifles personal growth.

The truth is nobody ever feels 100 percent ready when an opportunity arises, because most great opportunities in life force us to grow emotionally and intellectually. They force us to stretch ourselves and our comfort zones, which means we won't feel totally comfortable at first. And when we don't feel comfortable, we don't feel ready.

Just remember that significant moments of opportunity for personal growth and development will come and go throughout your lifetime. If you are looking to make positive changes in your life, you will need to embrace these moments of opportunity even though you will never feel 100 percent ready for them.

10 THINGS I Wish I Had KNOWN 10 Years Ago

STAY IN TUNE with your spirit. Be calm and think. Listen to your inner voice. Anticipate and plan. Take 100 percent responsibility for your life. I've learned these concepts gradually over the last decade. Together they have helped me live a life of purpose. Had I understood these things ten years ago, I could have avoided quite a bit of confusion and grief. So today I figured I'd share a few more things I wish I had known sooner. My hope is that they help you hurdle over some of the barriers I stumbled into on the road of life.

1. Loving someone should not mean losing you.

True love empowers you, it doesn't erase you. True love allows human beings to build amazing things, by working together through passion, kindness, and goodwill. So be strong enough to stand alone, be yourself enough to stand apart, but be wise enough to share your love and stand together when the time comes.

2. Getting even doesn't help you get ahead.

Sometimes we don't forgive people because they deserve it. We forgive them because they need it, because we need it, and because we cannot move forward without it. To forgive is to rediscover the inner peace and purpose that at first you thought someone took away when they betrayed you.

3. You attract what you show to the world.

So if you want it, reflect it. Happiness, freedom, and peace of mind are always attained by giving them out to others without expectation. The one who blesses others is abundantly blessed; those who help others are eventually helped.

4. Failure is success when you learn from it.

Experience is what you get when you don't get what you want. Obstacles can't stop you. Problems can't stop you. Other people can't stop you. These barriers are temporary—they come and go. Which is why, over the course of a lifetime, the only barrier that can truly stop you is *you*. So don't give up. Sometimes you have to journey through hell on Earth to find heaven on Earth.

5. You are not what you have done, but what you have overcome.

All the hardships. All the mistakes. All the rejections. All the pain. All the times you questioned why. All of these things have given birth to the wisdom and strength that will help you shine your light on the world, even in the darkest of hours.

6. Your past can only hurt you today if you let it.

The only way to get over the past is to leave it behind. If you spend your time reliving moments that are gone forever, you might miss the special moments that are yet to come.

7. It's never too late to become the person you are capable of being.

Repeat after me: *"I am free."* You can fulfill your life purpose by starting here, in this moment. The purpose of life is not to simply be happy, but to matter, to be productive, to be useful, to make some kind of difference that you have lived at all. Remember, life is constant change, but growth is optional. Choose wisely, starting now.

8. Passion is essential.

If you are trapped between your dreams and what other people think is right for you, always travel the route that makes you happy—unless you want everybody to be happy except you. And whatever you do, don't chase the money. Catch up to the ideas and activities that make you come alive. Go for the things of greater value—the things money can't buy—and use them to create a relevant profession.

9. The pain is worth it.

You can't really begin to appreciate life until it has knocked you down a few times. You can't really begin to appreciate love until your heart has been broken. You can't really begin to appreciate happiness until you've known sadness. You have to struggle up the mountainside to appreciate the breathtaking view at the top.

10. Sometimes what you don't want is what you need.

Sometimes the things you can't change end up changing you for the better. Master your responses to external events; don't always attempt to control them. You will rarely end up exactly where you wanted to go, but you will always end up exactly where you need to be.

12 LIFE LESSONS
Learned in 12 Years
on the Road

FOR MANY YEARS, we've been on the road—traveling (business and pleasure), studying, living in different cities, working for different companies (and ourselves), and meeting remarkable and unusual people everywhere in between. Here are twelve life lessons we've learned along the way:

1. Everyone has the same basic wants and needs.

When you get to know people with different ethnic backgrounds, from different cities and countries, who live at various socioeconomic levels, you begin to realize that everyone basically wants the same things. They want validation, love, happiness, fulfillment, and hopes for a better future. The way they pursue these desires is where things branch off, but the fundamentals are the same. You can relate to almost everyone everywhere if you look past the superficial façades that divide us.

2. What you do every day is what's most important.

The difference between who you are and who you want to be is what you do. You don't have to be great to get started, but you do have to get started to be great. Every accomplishment starts with the decision to try. Remember, people seldom do things to the best of their ability, they do things to the best of their willingness. Follow your heart, and do something every day that your future self will thank you for.

3. You can't always be agreeable.

That's how people take advantage of you. You have to set boundaries. Don't ever change just to impress someone. Change because it makes you a better person and leads you to a better future. Being your true self is the most effective formula for happiness and success there is. Sometimes you need to step outside, get some air, and remind yourself of who you are and what you want to be. And sometimes you just have to do your own thing your own way, no matter what anyone else thinks or says about you.

4. You're not perfect, but you're great at being you.

You might not be the most beautiful, the strongest, or the most talented person in the world, but that's OK. Don't pretend to be someone you're not. You're great at being you. You might not be proud of all the things you've done in the past, but that's OK too. The past is not today. Be proud of who you are, how you've grown, and what you've learned along the way.

5. You don't want perfect people in your life.

Even though you probably sometimes get confused, you don't really want your friends and lovers to be perfect. What you do want is people you can trust, who treat you right—people you can act silly with, who love being around you as much as you love being around them. It's about finding people who know about your mistakes and weaknesses and stand by your side when others walk away.

6. Life is change. You must embrace it.

Everything in life is temporary. So if things are good, enjoy it. It won't last forever. If things are bad, don't worry, because that won't last forever either. Just because life isn't easy right now doesn't mean you can't laugh. Just because something is bothering you doesn't mean you can't smile. Always focus on the positives in your life. You have a lot to look forward to. Every moment gives you a new beginning and a new ending. You get a second chance, every second.

7. Your scars are symbols of your growth.

Don't ever be ashamed of the scars life has left you with. A scar means the hurt is over and the wound is closed. It means you conquered the pain, learned a lesson, grew stronger, and moved on. A scar is the tattoo of a triumph to be proud of.

8. The truth is always the best choice.

Respect and trust are two of the easiest things in life to lose and the hardest to get back. Never make a big decision when you're angry, and never make a big promise when you're overjoyed. Never mess with someone's feelings just because you're unsure of yours. Always be open and honest.

9. It's the small, free things that matter most in life.

It's nice to have money and the things that money can buy, but it's also important to make sure you haven't lost track of the things that money can't buy. Maturity is not when you start speaking and thinking about the big things, it's when you start understanding and appreciating the small things.

10. Everyone's story is more complicated than it seems.

Every passing face on the street represents a story every bit as compelling and complicated as yours. It's not always the tears that measure a person's pain; sometimes it's the smile they fake. Not all scars show. Not all wounds heal by themselves. Don't judge a person negatively for their past or their feelings without a full understanding of their situation. And don't be so quick to point out the flaws in other people's lives when you are not willing to look at the flaws in your own life.

11. Giving up and moving on are two different things.

There is a difference between giving up and knowing when you have had enough. It doesn't make sense to hold on to something that's no longer there. Accepting what is, letting go, and moving on are skills that you must learn when facing the realities of life. Some relationships and situations just can't be fixed. If you try to force them back together, things will only get worse. Holding on is being brave, but letting go and moving on is often what makes us stronger.

12. You are not alone in being alone.

No matter how embarrassed you feel about your own situation, there are others out there experiencing the same emotions. There's always someone who can relate to you. Perhaps you can't talk to them right now, but they're out there.

Sometimes, changing your environment can shift your perspective. If you've been stuck in an emotional rut for a while, without any positive change, perhaps it's time to take a short hiatus—get out of town for a few days, experience something new, and stimulate your mind.

SIMPLICITY QUESTIONS
TO MAKE YOU THINK

What do you need to SPEND less *time* doing?

What makes you FEEL *comfortable*?

What's something SIMPLE that makes you *smile*?

What would you REGRET not *fully* doing, being, or having in your life?

When you're ninety years old, what will MATTER to you *most*?

The BEST part of *waking up* is _____?

What's one thing you LOVE about your *life*?

What would the CHILD you once were think of the *adult* you have become?

What's something you look FORWARD to almost *every day*?

What's something that makes you INSTANTLY feel *better*?

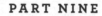

PART NINE

Inspiration

*Have an unrelenting belief that things will work out,
that the long road has a purpose, that the things
that you desire may not happen today,
but they are coming up over the horizon.*

THE SMARTEST CHOICE
WE CAN MAKE

The Only Way

My cell phone rang just after midnight. I didn't answer. Then it rang again a minute later. I rolled over, grabbed the phone off the nightstand, and squinted at the bright, glowing caller ID screen. "Claire," it read. Claire is a close friend—a friend who tragically lost her husband to a car accident six months ago. And I figured since she rarely calls me in the middle of the night, it was probably important.

"Hey, Claire. Is everything OK?" I asked.

"No!" she declared as she burst into tears. "I need to talk ... I need help ..."

"I'm listening," I reassured her. "What's on your mind?"

"I lost my job this evening, and I'm tired, and I just don't know anymore ..."

"A job is just a job. They come and go. Remember, Angel lost her job last year and it was a blessing in disguise. She found something better."

"I know, I know," she sighed over her tears, "I just felt like the world was going to end after the accident ... Ya know? And then my friends and family helped me get back on my feet ..."

"And you're still on your feet right now," I added.

"Well, sometimes I feel like I am, and sometimes I feel like I'm barely maintaining my balance, and sometimes I feel like I'm falling again. And this series of feelings just keeps cycling over and over again in a loop—good days followed by bad days and vice versa. It's just one long struggle. And I'm exhausted!"

"But you keep moving forward..."

"Actually," she continued over more tears, "the only way I've found to keep myself moving forward from moment to moment through the hard times is by repeating a short saying my grandfather taught me when I was a kid. And I don't know how or why it helps now, but it does."

"What's the saying?" I asked.

"'Do your best with what's in front of you and leave the rest to the powers above you,'" she replied.

I smiled, because I love inspirational ideas that help people progress through even the hardest of times. And because it suddenly reminded me of a short story my grandfather told me when I was a kid—one that's also applicable to Claire's circumstance.

"Your grandfather was a wise man," I said. "And it's funny, because your grandfather's saying reminds me of a short story my grandfather once told me. Would you like to hear it?"

"Yeah," she replied.

My Grandfather's Story

Once upon a time, in a small Indian village, the village fisherman accidentally dropped his favorite fishing pole into the river and was unable to retrieve it. When his neighbors caught word of his loss, they came over and said, "That's just bad luck!" The fisherman replied, "Perhaps."

The following day, the fisherman hiked a mile down the bank of the river to see if he could find his fishing pole. He came upon a small, calm cove in the riverbank that was loaded to the brim with salmon. He used a backup fishing pole to catch nearly a hundred salmon, loaded them into his wagon, and brought them back to the village to barter with other villagers. Everyone in the village was ecstatic to receive the fresh salmon. When his neighbors caught word of his success, they came over and said, "Wow! What great luck you have!" The fisherman replied, "Perhaps."

Two days later, the fisherman began hiking back toward the cove so he could catch more salmon. But a tenth of a mile into the hike, he tripped on a tree stump and severely sprained his ankle. He slowly and painfully hopped back to the village to nurse his health. When his neighbors caught word of his injury, they came over and said, "That's just bad luck!" The fisherman replied, "Perhaps."

Four days went by, and although the fisherman's ankle was slowly healing, he could not yet walk, and the village was completely out of fish to eat. Three other villagers volunteered to go to the river to fish while the fisherman recovered. That evening, when the three men did not return, the village sent a search party out for them only to discover that the men had been attacked and killed by a pack of wolves. When the fisherman's neighbors caught word of this, they came over and said, "You're so lucky you weren't out there fishing. What great luck you have!" The fisherman replied, "Perhaps."

"A few days later . . . well, you can guess how the story continues," I said.

The Moral of the Story

Claire chuckled and said, "Thank you." Because the moral of the story was immediately clear to her. We just don't know—we never do. Life is unpredictable. No matter how good or bad things seem right now, we can never be 100 percent certain what will happen next.

And this actually lifts a huge weight off our shoulders. Because it means that regardless of what's happening to us right now—good, bad, or indifferent—it's all just part of the phenomenon we call "life," which flows like the river in my grandfather's story, unpredictably from one occurrence to the next. And the smartest choice we can make is to swim with the flow of the river.

Which means, quite simply, not panicking in the face of unforeseen misfortunes or losing our poise in the limelight of our triumphs, but instead "doing our best with what's in front of us and leaving the rest to the powers above us."

10 THINGS You Should LEAVE in the Past

YOU MIGHT NOT be proud of all the things you've done in the past, but that's OK. The past is not today. Here are ten things to leave behind and grow beyond:

1. Letting other people write your life's story

You could spend your whole life worrying about what other people think of you, or what they want for you, but it won't get you very far. If you don't take charge and design your own life plan, chances are you'll fall into someone else's plan. And guess what they have planned for you? *Not much!*

2. The fear of making mistakes

Often our greatest achievements and our most beautiful creations emerge from the emotions we live, the lessons we learn, and the messes we make along the way. Just ask a poet, an artist, a songwriter, a lover, or a parent; in the long run, things rarely turn out as planned, just better than you ever imagined.

3. The belief that "perfect" means the same thing to everyone

Perfect people come from every corner of this beautiful planet and can be seen everywhere—even in the mirror. Yeah, that's right! Perfect is the way we are born. Perfect is the way we are now. Perfect is unique. We are all perfect just the way we are.

4. Negative thinking

It is our thoughts that really dictate the way we feel, so why not choose thoughts that make you feel amazing? The more you praise and celebrate your life, the more there is in life to celebrate. You can choose to make the rest of your life the best of your life.

5. Doing something just because others are

Give yourself permission to immediately walk away from anything that gives you bad vibes. There is no need to explain or make sense of it. Just trust what you feel.

6. Not following your intuition

One day your life will flash before your eyes; make sure it's worth watching. Stop and think about it. Really think about it. What is it that you really want to do with your life? Forget what you think you should do. What excites you? What feels impossible? Be honest with yourself. Your answers don't need to make an impression on anyone but you.

7. Procrastinating on your goals and passions

The difference between who you are and who you want to be is what you do. Yes, it will hurt. It will take time. It will require dedication. It will require willpower. You will need to make healthy decisions. It will require sacrifice. You will need to push your mind and body to their max. There will be temptation. But I promise you, when you reach your goal, it will be worth it. And remember, nothing you have passion for is ever a waste of time, no matter how it turns out.

8. The belief that failure is the opposite of success

Failure is not the opposite of success, it is part of success. Failure becomes success when we learn from it. If you change the way you look at things, the things you look at change. Instead of looking at what's missing, and how far you still have to go, focus on what's present, and how far you have come.

9. People who want you to be someone else

Never change who you are. Be yourself. People will love you for it, and if they don't, let them go.

10. People who are already gone

There are no failed relationships, because every person in your life has a lesson to teach. Sometimes you simply outgrow people. Don't try to fix the unfixable, just accept it and move on. When someone leaves you, it's important to emotionally release them. And know it's not an ending— it's a new beginning. It just means that their part in your story is over. Your story will go on.

18 THINGS I Wish SOMEONE Had Told Me When I Was 18

RECENTLY I WAS reading a book at my favorite beachside coffee shop when an eighteen-year-old kid sat down next to me and said, "That's a great read, ain't it?" So we started chatting.

He told me he was getting ready to graduate from high school in a couple of weeks and then immediately starting his college career in the fall. "But I have no clue what I want to do with my life," he said. "Right now I'm just going with the flow."

And then, with eager, honest eyes, he began asking me one question after the next:

"What do you do for a living?"

"When and how did you decide what you wanted to do?"

"Why did you do this? Why didn't you do that?"

"Is there anything you wish you had done differently?"

I answered his questions as best I could, and tried to give decent advice with the time I had. After a half-hour conversation, he thanked me and we parted ways.

But on the walk home, I realized the conversation I had with him was actually quite nostalgic for me. He reminded me of me at that age. So I started thinking about his questions again, and I began imagining all of the things I wish someone had told me when I was eighteen.

Then I took it a step further and thought about all the things I would love to tell myself if I could travel back in time to give my eighteen-year-old self some advice about life.

So after a few cups of coffee and a couple hours of deliberation, here are eighteen things I wish someone had told me when I was eighteen:

1. Commit yourself to making lots of mistakes.

Sometimes the wrong choices bring us to the right places. So don't worry about mistakes; worry about what you're giving up when you don't try. Worry about the life you're not allowing yourself to live! No book is one chapter long. No chapter tells the whole story. No mistake defines who we are. Keep turning the pages that need to be turned.

2. Find hard work you love doing.

If I could offer my eighteen-year-old self some real career advice, I'd tell myself not to base my career choice on other people's ideas, goals, and recommendations. I'd tell myself not to pick a major because it's popular, or statistically creates graduates who make the most money. I'd tell myself that the right career choice is based on one key point: finding hard work you love doing. As long as you remain true to yourself, and follow your own interests and values, you can find success through passion. Perhaps more important, you won't wake up several years later working in a career field you despise, wondering, "How the heck am I going to do this for the next thirty years?" So if you catch yourself working hard and loving every minute of it, don't stop. You're onto something big. Because hard work ain't hard when you concentrate on your passions.

3. Invest time, energy, and money in yourself every day.

When you invest in yourself, you can never lose, and over time you will change the trajectory of your life. You are simply the product of what you know. The more time, energy, and money you spend acquiring pertinent knowledge, the more control you have over your life.

4. Explore new ideas and opportunities often.

Your natural human fears of failure and embarrassment will sometimes stop you from trying new things. But you must rise above these fears, for your life's story is simply the culmination of many small, unique experiences. And the more unique experiences you have, the more interesting your story gets. So seek as many new life experiences as possible and be sure to share them with the people you care about. Not doing so is not living.

5. When sharpening your career skills, focus more on less.

Hard work matters, but not if it's scattered in diverse directions. So narrow your focus on learning fewer career-related skills and master them all.

6. People are not mind readers. Tell them what you're thinking.

People will never know how you feel unless you tell them. Your boss? He doesn't know you're hoping for a promotion, because you haven't told him yet. That cute girl you haven't talked to because you're too shy? Yeah, you guessed it: she hasn't given you the time of day simply because you haven't given her the time of day either. In life, you have to communicate with others. It's as simple as that.

7. Make swift decisions and take immediate action.

Either you're going to take action and seize new opportunities, or someone else will first. You can't change anything or make any sort of progress by sitting back and thinking about it. Remember, there's a huge difference between knowing how to do something and actually doing it. Knowledge is basically useless without action.

8. Accept and embrace change.

However good or bad a situation is now, it will change. That's the one thing you can count on. So embrace change, and realize that change happens for a reason. It won't always be easy or obvious at first, but in the end it will be worth it.

9. Don't worry too much about what other people think about you.

For the most part, what other people think and say about you doesn't matter. When I was eighteen, I let the opinions of my high school and early college peers influence my decisions. And, at times, they steered me away from ideas and goals I strongly believed in. I realize now that this was a foolish way to live, especially when I consider that nearly all of these people whose opinions I cared so much about are no longer a part of my life. Unless you're trying to make a great first impression (job interview, first date), don't let the opinions of others stand in your way. What they think and say about you isn't important. What is important is how you feel about yourself.

10. Always be honest with yourself and others.

Living a life of honesty creates peace of mind, and peace of mind is priceless. Period.

11. Talk to lots of people in college and early on in your career.

Bosses. Colleagues. Professors. Classmates. Social club members. Other students outside of your major or social circle. Teaching assistants. Career advisors. College deans. Friends of friends. Everyone! Why? Professional networking. Over time, you'll continue talking to new people you meet through your current network and your network's reach, and the associated opportunities will continue to snowball for the duration of your career.

12. Sit alone in silence for at least ten minutes every day.

Use this time to think, plan, reflect, and dream. Creative and productive thinking flourish in solitude and silence. With quiet, you can hear your thoughts, you can reach deep within yourself, and you can focus on mapping out the next logical, productive step in your life.

13. Ask lots of questions.

The greatest "adventure" is the ability to inquire, to ask questions. Sometimes in the process of inquiry, the search is more significant than the answers. Answers come from other people, from the universe of knowledge and history, and from the intuition and deep wisdom inside yourself. These answers will never surface if you never ask the right questions. Ask.

14. Exploit the resources you do have access to.

Too often, we don't make the connections, ask the questions, and pursue the opportunities in front of us. Brainstorm. Make lists. Do the most you can with what you have—and prepare to pay it forward too.

15. Live below your means.

Live a comfortable life, not a wasteful one. Do not live life trying to fool yourself into thinking wealth is measured in material objects. Always live well below your means.

16. Be respectful of others and make them feel good.

In life and business, it's not so much what you say that counts, it's how you make people feel. So respect your elders, minors, and everyone in between. Supporting, guiding, and making contributions to other people is one of life's greatest rewards.

17. Excel at what you do.

There's no point in doing something if you aren't going to do it right. Excel at your work and excel at your hobbies. Develop a reputation for consistent excellence.

18. Be who you were born to be.

Regardless of what you decide to do in your lifetime, you'd better feel it in every fiber of your being. You'd better be born to do it! Don't waste your life fulfilling someone else's dreams and desires.

Above all, laugh when you can, apologize when you should, and let go of what you can't change. Life is short, yet amazing. Enjoy the ride.

12 THINGS My GRANDMOTHER Told Me Before She Died

WHEN MY GRANDMOTHER Zelda passed away a few years ago at the age of ninety, she left me with a box of miscellaneous items from her house that she knew I had grown to appreciate over the years. Among these items is an old leather-bound volume that she aptly named her "Inspiration Journal."

Throughout the second half of her life, she used this journal to jot down ideas, thoughts, quotes, song lyrics, and anything else that moved her. She would read excerpts from her journal to me when I was growing up, and I would listen and ask questions. I honestly credit a part of who I am now to the wisdom she bestowed on me when I was young.

Today I want to share some of these inspiring excerpts with you. I've done my best to sort, copyedit, and reorganize the content into twelve inspiring points. Enjoy.

1. Breathe in the future, breathe out the past.

No matter where you are or what you're going through, always believe that there is a light at the end of the tunnel. Never expect, assume, or demand. Just do your best, control the elements you can control, and then let it be. Because once you have done what you can, if it is meant to be, it will happen, or it will show you the next step that needs to be taken.

2. Life can be simple again.

Just choose to focus on one thing at a time. You don't have to do it all, and you don't have to do it all right now. Breathe, be present, and do your best with what's in front of you.

3. Let others accept you as you are, or not at all.

Speak your truth even if your voice shakes. By being yourself, you put something beautiful into the world that was not there before. So walk your path confidently and don't expect anyone else to understand your journey, especially if they have not been exactly where you are going.

4. You are not who you used to be, and that's OK.

Over the years, so many things have happened—things that have changed your perspective, taught you lessons, and forced your spirit to grow. As time passes, nobody stays the same, but some people will still tell you that you have changed. Respond to them by saying, "Of course I've changed. But I'm still the same person, just a little stronger now than I ever was before."

5. Everything that happens helps you grow, even if it's hard to see right at first.

Circumstances will direct you, correct you, and perfect you over time. So whatever you do, hold on to hope. The tiniest thread will twist into an unbreakable cord. Let hope anchor you in the possibility that this is not the end of your story—that the change in the tides will eventually bring you to peaceful shores.

6. Do not educate yourself to be rich—educate yourself to be happy.

That way when you get older you'll know the value of things, not the price. In the end, you will come to realize that the best days are the days when you don't need anything extreme or special to happen to make you smile. You simply appreciate the moments and feel gratitude, seeking nothing else, nothing more. That's what true happiness is all about.

7. Be determined to stay positive.

Understand that the greater part of your unhappiness is determined not by your circumstances, but by your attitude. So smile at those who often try to begrudge or hurt you; show them what's missing in their life and what they can't take away from you.

8. Pay close attention to those you care about.

Sometimes when a loved one says, "I'm OK," they need you to look them in the eyes, hug them tight, and reply, "I know you're not." And don't be too upset if some people only seem to remember you when they need you. Feel privileged that you are like a beacon of light that comes to their mind when there is darkness in their life.

9. Sometimes you have to let a person go so they can grow.

Over the course of their lives, it is not what you do for them, but what you have taught them to do for themselves that will make them a successful human being.

10. Sometimes getting the results you crave means stripping yourself of people who don't serve your best interests.

This allows you to make space for those who support you in being the absolute best version of yourself. It happens gradually as you grow. You find out who you are and what you want, and then you realize that people you've known forever don't see things the way you do. So you keep the wonderful memories, but find yourself moving on.

11. It's better to look back on life and say, "I can't believe I did that," than to look back and say, "I wish I had done that."

In the end, people will judge you in some way anyway. So don't live your life trying to impress others. Instead, live your life impressing yourself. Love yourself enough to never lower your standards for anyone.

12. If you're looking for a happy ending, maybe it's time to start looking for a new beginning.

Brush yourself off and accept that you have to fail from time to time. That's how you learn. The strongest people out there—the ones who laugh the hardest with a genuine smile—are the same people who have fought the toughest battles. They're smiling because they've decided that they're not going to let anything hold them down, they're moving on to a new beginning.

WHY I LIVE EVERY DAY LIKE IT'S MY LAST

A Good Girl

Alyssa was my best friend. She was a talented musician, a graceful gymnast, a brilliant writer, and a deeply passionate individual. She cared so much about people. Love oozed from every facet of her being. When she spoke, her eyes were as sincere as her words. And she always wanted to understand what was wrong so she could strive to make it better.

But Alyssa woke up one day during her senior year in college with a strange pain in her chest. The on-campus doctors didn't understand why, so they referred her to a specialist. After several MRIs and blood tests, they determined that she had a rare, escalated case of Hodgkin's lymphoma—a form of cancer. She spent the next three years suffering through varying degrees of pain and sickness as multiple doctors treated her with radiation and chemotherapy. And although these doctors were initially hopeful, Alyssa's condition worsened, and she eventually passed away on her twenty-fifth birthday.

A Bad Guy

Ethan was also my friend. Though not as multitalented as Alyssa, he was insanely smart—particularly when it came to money and business. But he didn't care about people. I eventually learned, just before ending our eight-year friendship, that he ripped people off for a living. He primarily targeted elderly folks who had relatively small life savings. "They're all suckers," he told me. And he felt no remorse because, he continued, "they'll be dead soon anyway."

Today, at the age of twenty-eight, Ethan is a multimillionaire. And although we haven't spoken in years, I've heard from others that he still hasn't gotten into any legal trouble—largely, I think, because of the calculated threats that I've heard he makes to anyone he suspects might have a good conscience. I hear, also, that he doesn't suffer from any major health problems, and that he, his trophy wife, and his two healthy sons live in a mansion somewhere in Southern California.

The Reason

These are old stories—familiar stories. The people and the circumstances differ slightly for everyone who tells them, but the core lessons remain the same. Life isn't fair. Bad things do happen to good people. And good things do happen to bad people.

Yet these are the excuses many of us use when we choose not to follow our hearts. And they are the excuses many of us use when we choose to treat ourselves and each other without dignity and respect. "Why care," we argue, "when the Alyssas of the world suffer and die young while the Ethans of the world sip wine at five-star resorts well into their eighties?"

But for some of us, Alyssa and Ethan are the reason we do follow our hearts. His story is the reason we live to make the world a little brighter, to make people a little happier. And her story is the reason we use all of the strength we have right now. Because we know we may not have the same strength tomorrow.

Because a world with no guarantees requires us to live every day . . . as if it were our last.

9 THINGS No One Wants to REGRET When They're Older

RIGHT NOW WE have an opportunity to change our future. Right now we can choose to erase regret from our later years. Here are nine things none of us wants to regret when we're older, and some thoughts on avoiding these regrets:

1. Not spending enough time smiling with the people you love

When your work life is busy, and all your energy is focused in that arena, it's all too easy to find yourself off balance. While drive and focus are important, if you intend to maintain happiness and peace in your life, you still need to balance in the soccer games, the family dinners, the intimate dates with your significant other, and more.

2. Holding a grudge

Grudges are a waste of perfect happiness. If there's someone in your life who deserves another chance, give it to them. If you need to apologize, do it. Give your story together a happy new beginning.

3. Fulfilling everyone else's dreams instead of your own

Unfortunately, just before you take your first step on the righteous journey to pursue your dreams, people around you, even the ones who deeply care for you, will likely give you bad advice. It's because they don't understand the big picture—what your dreams, passions, and life goals mean to you. Have the courage to live a life true to *you*, not the life others expect of you. Make time to pursue your passion, no matter what anyone else says.

4. Not being honest about how you feel

Many people suppress their feelings in order to keep peace with others. As a result, they settle for carrying the weight of their own silence. Give yourself permission to feel a full range of emotions. When you're in touch with what you're feeling, you're more likely to understand the situation at hand and resolve it instead of avoiding it. In the end, expressing your feelings will boost your relationships, including your relationship with yourself, to a new, healthier level.

5. Being irresponsible with your finances

When you spend less than you make, you buy lifestyle flexibility and freedom. You are buying the ability to say yes to the things that matter, because you're saving on the things that don't. Manage your money wisely so your money does not manage you.

6. Getting caught up in needless drama and negativity

Staying out of other people's drama is an incredibly effective way to simplify your life and reduce stress. Surround yourself with positive people who make you laugh so hard that you forget the bad and focus on the good.

7. Spending time with people who make you unhappy

To find true happiness in life, you have to follow your heart and intuition. You have to be who you are, and design a lifestyle and career that fulfills you—no matter what that entails or what people say about it. Life isn't about pleasing everybody. Begin today by taking responsibility for your own happiness. You are the only one who can create it. The choice is yours.

8. Never making a difference in the lives of others

Do something that's greater than you—something that helps someone else to be happy or to suffer less. Remember, making a positive difference in one person's life can change the world. Maybe not the whole world, but certainly theirs.

9. Failing because you were scared to fail

If you find yourself at a point of intense decision making where you're caught in a spiral of overanalysis and hesitation, and you're making no progress, take a deep breath, break the spiral, make an educated guess on the next logical step, and take it. Even if you get it wrong, you will learn something that will help you get it right next time.

30 TRUTHS I've Learned in 30 YEARS

THESE ARE SIMPLE lessons about life in general that I picked up while traveling, living in different cities, working for different companies (and myself), and meeting remarkable and unusual people everywhere in between.

1. There comes a point in life when you get tired of chasing everyone and trying to fix everything, but it's not giving up. It's realizing you don't need certain people and things and the drama they bring.

2. You can't control how other people feel, or how they receive your energy. Anything you do or say gets filtered through a mind-set occupied by whatever they are going through at the moment, which has nothing to do with you. Just keep doing your thing with as much love as possible.

3. If a person wants to be a part of your life, they will make an obvious effort to do so. Don't bother reserving a space in your heart for people who do not make an effort to stay.

4. If you want to fly, you have to give up the things that weigh you down—which is not always as obvious and easy as it sounds.

5. Doing something and getting it wrong is at least ten times more productive than doing nothing.

6. Every success has a trail of failures behind it, and every failure is leading toward success. You don't fail by falling down. You fail by never getting back up. Sometimes you just have to forget how you feel, remember what you deserve, and keep pushing forward.

7. The more things you own, the more your things own you. Less truly gives you more freedom.

8. While you're busy looking for the perfect person, you'll probably miss the imperfect person who could make you perfectly happy. This is as true for friendships as it is for intimate relationships. Finding a companion or a friend isn't about trying to transform yourself into the perfect image of what you think they want. It's about being exactly who you are and then finding someone who appreciates that.

9. Relationships must be chosen wisely. It's better to be alone than to be in bad company. If something is meant to be, it will happen—in the right time, with the right person, and for the best reason.

10. Making a hundred friends is not a miracle. A miracle is making one friend who will stand by your side when hundreds have walked away.

11. Someone will always be better looking. Someone will always be smarter. Someone will always be more charismatic. But they will never be you—with your exact ideas, knowledge, and skills.

12. Making progress involves risk. Period. You can't make it to second base with your foot on first.

13. Every morning you are faced with two choices: you can aimlessly stumble through the day not knowing what's going to happen and simply react to events at a moment's notice, or you can go through the day directing your own life and making your own decisions and destiny.

14. Everyone makes mistakes. If you can't forgive others, don't expect others to forgive you. Set yourself free by forgiving someone else.

15. It's OK to fall apart for a little while. You don't always have to pretend to be strong, and there is no need to constantly prove that everything is going well. Cry if you need to—it's healthy to shed your tears. The sooner you do, the sooner you will be able to smile again.

16. We sometimes do things that are permanently foolish just because we are temporarily upset. A lot of heartache can be avoided if you learn to control your emotions.

17. Someone else doesn't have to be wrong for you to be right. You have to allow people to make their own mistakes and their own decisions.

18. Nobody has it easy. Every one of us has issues. So don't belittle yourself or anyone else. Everybody is fighting their own unique war.

19. A smile doesn't always mean a person is happy. Sometimes it simply means they are strong enough to face their problems.

20. The happiest people I know keep an open mind to new ideas and ventures, use their leisure time as a means of mental development, and love good music, good books, good pictures, good company, and good conversation. And oftentimes they are also the cause of happiness in others—me in particular.

21. You can't take things too personally. Rarely do people do things because of *you*. They do things because of *them*.

22. Feelings change, people change, and time keeps rolling on. You can hold on to past mistakes or you can create your own happiness. Don't make the mistake of waiting on someone or something to come along and make you happy.

23. It's much harder to change the length of your life than it is to change the depth of it.

24. You end up regretting the things you did *not* do far more than the things you did.

25. When you stop chasing the wrong things, you give the right things a chance to catch you.

26. One of the greatest challenges in life is being yourself in a world that's trying to make you the same as everyone else.

27. Enjoy the little things, because they're bigger than they first appear.

28. Anyone can make a difference. You have more power than you think. Use it.

29. Every experience is a life lesson—everyone you meet, everything you encounter. Never forget to acknowledge the lesson, especially when things don't go your way. Gain insight and move forward.

30. Regardless of how dark your past has been, your future is still spotless. Don't start your day with the broken pieces of yesterday. Each day is a new beginning. Every morning you wake up is the first day of the rest of your life. What do you want to make happen?

10 TIMELESS Lessons from a Life Well Lived

EARLIER IN THIS book we shared a list called "18 Things My Dad Was Right About." Recently, my dad e-mailed me an addendum to his original list. It contains ten additional life lessons from the smartest grandfather I know. Enjoy.

1. Happiness cannot be traveled to, owned, earned, worn, or consumed.

Happiness is the sacred experience of living every moment with love and gratitude. There is always, always, always something to be thankful for and some reason to love. So be sure to appreciate what you've got.

2. Be a student of life every day.

Experience it, learn from it, and absorb all the knowledge you can. Prepare yourself for greatness by keeping your mind conditioned with fresh knowledge and new challenges. Remember, if you stay ready, you won't have to prepare when great opportunities arise.

3. Experience is the best teacher.

Don't try too hard to memorize the things others are teaching. Learn the best practices and then do your thing. Life itself will teach you over the course of time, and often at the right time and place, so that you will remember forever what is truly important.

4. Your choices, your actions, your life.

Never let the odds keep you from doing what you know in your heart you were meant to do. Continue to work hard at what you love, no matter what the challenges are. Stay persistent. Life eventually rewards those who are.

5. No one is "too busy." It's all about priorities.

What you focus on grows. Don't say you don't have enough time. You have the same number of hours per day that were given to Helen Keller, Michelangelo, Mother Teresa, Leonardo da Vinci, Thomas Jefferson, Albert Einstein, and everyone around you.

6. Be patient and tough. Someday this pain will be useful to you.

Pain is a wake-up call that guides us toward a better future. So keep your heart open to dreams, and make that change. For as long as there is a dream and positive action, there is hope—and as long as there is hope, there is joy in living.

7. It's usually better to be kind than to be right.

Be kind whenever possible. And realize that it is always possible. It takes a great deal of strength to be gentle and kind. Sometimes the best thing to say is nothing at all—and to simply listen instead.

8. You can become a magnet for good things by wishing everyone well.

Judge less and love more. If you want inner peace, resist the temptation to gossip about others, or portray them in a poor light. Instead of judging someone for what they do or where they are in their life, figure out why they do what they do and how they got to where they are.

9. Only you are in charge of your attitude.

The truth is, unless you let go, unless you forgive yourself, unless you forgive the situation, unless you realize that that situation is over, you cannot move forward. You are responsible for how you feel, no matter what anyone else says or does. You are always 100 percent in control of your thoughts right now, so choose to feel confident and adequate rather than angry and insecure. Choose to look forward, not back.

10. Satisfaction is not always the fulfillment of what you want.

It is the realization of how blessed you are for what you have. It's not that everything will be easy or exactly as you had expected, but you must choose to be grateful for all that you have, and happy that you got a chance to live this life, no matter how it turns out.

INSPIRATIONAL QUESTIONS
TO MAKE YOU THINK

What does the CHILD inside you *long* for?

What is one thing right NOW that you are totally *sure* of?

What's the BEST *decision* you've ever made?

What is the BIGGEST *motivator* in your life right now?

What are you MOST *grateful* for?

What have you been COUNTING or *keeping track* of recently?

What's the difference between being ALIVE and truly *living*?

If you had the OPPORTUNITY to get a message across to a large group of people, what would your *message* be?

Have you DONE anything lately worth *remembering*?

When is the LAST time you tried something *new*?

Final Note

WE KNOW YOU'RE reading this. And we want you to know we're writing this for you. Others will be confused. They will think we're writing this for them. But we're not.

This one's for you.

We want you to know that life is not easy. Every day is an unpredictable challenge. Some days it can be difficult simply to get out of bed in the morning. To face reality and put on that smile. But we want you to know, your smile has kept us going on more days than we can count. Never forget that, even through the toughest times, you are incredible. You really are.

So smile more often. You have so many reasons to. Time and again, our reason is you.

You won't always be perfect. Neither will we. Because nobody is perfect, and nobody deserves to be perfect. Nobody has it easy, everybody has issues. You will never know exactly what we're going through. And we will never know exactly what you're going through. We are all fighting our own unique war.

But we are fighting through it simultaneously, together.

Remember, our courage doesn't always roar aloud. Sometimes it's the quiet voice at the end of the day whispering, "I will try again tomorrow." So stand strong. Things turn out best for people who make the best out of the way things turn out.

And we are committed to making the best of it along with you.

If You Want to Continue
Your Journey with Us

THE GETTING BACK TO HAPPY course is an online, self-paced course designed to help you take what you've learned in this book to the next level, with included one-on-one (and two-on-one) coaching directly from us.

Getting Back to Happy is the go-to course for anyone serious about taking action to reclaim their happiness and realize their potential. It will help you wake up every day and live with a fuller sense of purpose, even if you've tried everything else. If you've been wanting a way to work with us, this is it. It's the result of more than a decade of study and one-on-one coaching with hundreds of people just like you from all over the world. It's a proven system that works time and again to bust people out of their ruts and get them back on track to living a life they are excited about. From proven ways to foster stronger relationships to actions engineered to help you let go of painful emotions, the learning modules in this course will inspire and equip you to become your best self.

When you enroll in Getting Back to Happy, you'll receive access to a massive collection of helpful resources. From inspiring stories to actionable strategies to lots of live-engagement opportunities (phone calls and video calls) with us, Getting Back to Happy provides more than just great content: it fosters an uplifting community. Everyone who enrolls in Getting Back to Happy will get lifetime access to a supportive community and self-paced online course that's packed with sixty HD video trainings, including hundreds of scientifically proven methods for getting back on track, and members-only discussion forums where you can discuss each lesson with both of us and other course members.

LEARN MORE ABOUT Getting Back to Happy and enroll at marcandangel .com/getting-back-to-happy.

THE THINK BETTER, Live Better live conference is the go-to event for you if you're serious about taking action to reclaim your happiness and realize your true potential. Think Better, Live Better is designed to help you wake up every day and live life with a full sense of purpose, even if you've tried everything else. If you want to attend a life-changing conference filled with world-class personal development experts who care, this is it!

Think Better, Live Better is packed full of practical strategies and unforgettably inspiring lessons for living a more positive and productive life. But this is more than just an event. It's an immersive experience that will give you proven tools to identify and transform the negative, self-limiting beliefs and behaviors that keep you stuck. From proven ways to foster healthier relationships, to actions engineered to help you let go of painful experiences and emotions, to rituals guaranteed to increase your productivity, the actionable talks and workshops at this event—delivered by some of the brightest minds in personal growth—will inspire and equip you to become your most effective self.

This event is your gateway to the life you've planned on living. You won't leave Think Better, Live Better with a notebook full of ideas and nothing checked off your to-do list. Instead, you'll set into motion a realistic plan you can keep improving on for years to come. We will guide you step-by-step through mental-strength exercises, and help you refocus your mind on the powerful truths that will have the fastest and most effective impact on your personal and professional desires and goals.

Learn more and register for the next event at thinklivebetter.com.

About the Authors

credit Zaitogaphy

Passionate writers, admirers of the human spirit, and full-time students of life, Marc and Angel Chernoff enjoy sharing inspirational advice and practical tips for life on their popular personal development blog, *Marc and Angel Hack Life.* Currently the site contains about six hundred articles on productivity, happiness, love, work, and general self-improvement, and has attracted seventy million page views since its inception in the summer of 2006. They are authors of the *New York Times* bestseller *Getting Back to Happy.*

Marc and Angel both share a great passion for inspiring others to live to their fullest potential, and they honestly feel best when they are inspiring others to be their best. They started their blog with the goal of inspiring as many people as possible. And they work passionately every day to fulfill this goal through the thoughts and ideas they share online.

Please catch up with them at marcandangel.com.

Or you can e-mail them: angel@marcandangel.com and marc@marcandangel.com.

Subscribe for Free

If you have enjoyed this book and found it useful, you will love all the other articles at Marc and Angel Hack Life. Readers continually leave feedback on how they have benefited tremendously from the site's material and how it's a staple for their personal growth.

By *subscribing*, you will receive free practical tips and inspirational advice geared for productive living, served fresh three times a week directly to your inbox: marcandangel. com/subscribe.

LET'S CONNECT

We would love to hear from you and to know what you think. Feel free to get in touch with us via the following channels:

facebook.com/marcandangelhacklife
twitter.com/marcandangel
instagram.com/marcandangel

GUEST POST

"5 Character Traits That Make You Happy," by Ken Wert of Meant to Be Happy

Also by Marc & Angel Chernoff

tarcherperigee

An imprint of Penguin Random House
penguinrandomhouse.com
tarcherperigee.com